the TALE gets LONGER

a sequel to
A LIE IN THE TALE

JOHN (*JACK*) ALEXANDER

The Tale Gets Longer © 2025 John Alexander

All Rights Reserved. No part of this book may be reproduced in any form or by any electronic or mechanical means including information storage and retrieval systems, without permission in writing from the author. The only exception is by a reviewer, who may quote short excerpts in a review.

No generative artifical intelligence (AI) was used in the creation of this book. The author expressly prohibits the use of this publication as training data for AI technologies or large language models (LLMs) for generative purposes. The author reserves all rights to license uses of this work for generative AI training and the development of LLMs.

This book is a work of non-fiction. This publication is designed to provide accurate and authoritative information in regards to the subject matter covered. It is sold with the understanding that neither the author nor the publisher is engaged in rendering legal, investment, accounting, or other professional services. For privacy reasons, some names, locations, and dates may have been changed.

These are the memories of the author, from their perspective, and they have tried to represent events as faithfully as possible.

Printed in Australia

Cover and internal design by Coven Press

www.covenpress.com.au

Images in this book are copyright approved for use by author

First printing: June 2025

Paperback ISBN 978-1-7640189-0-6

eBook ISBN 978-1-7640189-1-3

 A catalogue record for this work is available from the National Library of Australia

Distributed by Lightning Source Global

To Damon and Deborah
The two children of very proud parents.

C.1

A New Start

Employment, Aircraft, Heat and Flies

A chance meeting, a life changed forever. It happened in Melbourne. Hang on, didn't I leave Melbourne as a teenager to be a jackaroo in Queensland? Which, I might add, was quite successful.

Before my life changed forever, there is a story to tell.

It was just an ordinary house with a picket fence, just down the street from the Royal Hotel in Goondiwindi, which, if you didn't know, is a country town on the border of Queensland and NSW. Now, this ordinary house was a boarding house, in fact, Thompson's boarding house, run by Mrs Thompson, her daughter, who was a shearer's cook and her son, a shearer. They were big people, rough, but kind and friendly. They ran a clean and excellent establishment. I would often stay there.

The clientele were mostly shearers who stayed between sheds, a few bank johnnies and an ex-jackaroo who was looking for some shearing. That was me, Jack. You might have heard of me in my first book, "A Lie in the Tale".

The house was partitioned into small rooms, giving everyone

their own space. A small kitchen, a dining room, which would be better described as an eating room, which had a long table for eight to 10 enthusiastic, hungry eaters, who always enjoyed good hearty meals, supplied by Mrs Thompson and her adult children.

Staying there for a couple of weeks, getting odd jobs, helping cement the town bore, which was mainly me shovelling sand and gravel into a large cement mixer. Then a few days here and there, doing a bit of "straggler" shearing. That's what I wanted to do, shearing, to earn big money so I could ask my girl from Lota to marry me. We had agreed to a separation of 12 months for me to get a bank together and see how strong our love was for each other.

It was too early in the year for the big shearing sheds to start, so I grabbed any job that came my way. Sunday arvo, reading The Queensland Country Life newspaper situations vacant column, I spied this ad, "Wanted Experienced Stockman. Immediately for large sheep and cattle property, Julia Creek Area, $33 clear a week plus food and board."

There was a phone number to ring. Wow, $33 a week, and my last job as a jackaroo was $15. I decided to ring that number in the morning.

"Yes, the manager of Lindfield Station is looking for a stockman urgently," said the agent.

"Is it right that the wage is $132 a month?" I asked. All wages were paid monthly.

"Yes, that's correct and its fully found, are you interested?"

I wasn't game to say, "I'll think about it," as I might have missed out, so I said, "Yes."

"Then I will inform them. May I have your full name, address and contact number? I will be in touch." He then hung up. I did not get his name or ask where Julia Creek was. Well, I'd done it now. I better find out where this Julia Creek was.

I asked Rodney, one of my fellow boarders. He said it was way up in the gulf country in Northern Queensland. Mrs Thompson lent me her Queensland map. Julia Creek was about 2,500 kilometres from Goondiwindi.

"I don't know. It's a long way to get a job. How do I get there? Will I have to pay a fare? Can I back out?"

Later that afternoon, Mrs Thompson said, "I have a message for you."

Reading from the note in her hand, with the spectacles on her nose, she said, "Mr Sailen will meet you at Gannon's Hotel, Julia Creek at 6:30pm this Friday."

"Is that all? Help, how am I going to get there this week?"

"Fly, I guess. I think, first thing in the morning Jack you should see one of the agents and they should be able to organise your travel plans. It will be a long trip so good luck."

All I could say was, "Thanks a lot."

I was restless that night, then at 8.30 in the morning, I walked down the street to the stock and station Dalgety's office and saw Mrs Gillespie at reception, and said, "My name is Jack and I have a bit of a problem, I have just got a job at Julia Creek and must be there by 6.30 this Friday, is it possible you could arrange to get me there and what would it cost? Is that something you could help me with?"

"Well young man you have some travelling to do. I will see what I can arrange. It could be difficult, but I can try. Could you call back at 11:00 this morning?"

"Yeah, thanks a lot, but is it possible and how much will it cost?"

"Well, I hope to answer all your questions when you come back, Jack, but I think I might be able to manage something."

I said a big thankyou and left with a worried smile.

Next stop was the café for a choc malt and a cream bun to settle some butterflies in my stomach. Why do I always jump into something without first doing a bit of homework or research as to what the consequences could be? I suppose mystery and problem solving are a couple of my virtues.

I could not wait any longer, I went to the agents at 10.45 to see what I had got myself in for. Walking in and saying "G'day" to Mrs Gillespie I asked, "Have you found out anything yet?"

"Oh yes, Jack. I have the information you require but it won't be all plain sailing. Now, I have it all down here." She shuffled some typewritten papers and said, "Well, I hope you're ready to travel first thing in the morning.

"The Skinner Bus leaves here at 9am and arrives in Brisbane at 2pm. You will need accommodation for two nights and then, from Eagle Farm, a TAA aircraft to Townsville and then another aircraft, probably ANA, to Julie Creek.

"The trip leaves 10am Friday morning and arrives at Julia Creek at 6pm so it is quite the trip, but you will get there.

"Now Jack, if you can afford it, we can book the bus and the plane and pay the fares for you, but we will need the money now."

"Hum," said I with the tightening of the throat muscles, "how much do you think I will need?"

"That's $10 for the bus and $120 for the plane fare. Jack, that's a whopping $130.00. Have you got that?"

I suddenly had trouble standing up, as I seemed to contract the syndrome of weak knees.

"Can you hang on for about an hour? As I will have to go to the bank to see If I can afford to pay the money."

"Yes, Jack, but the sooner you get back, the sooner I can have it all arranged for you."

I had paid Mrs Thompson for board, so that was taken care of. I didn't have to go to the bank, I just went to my room and checked out my Commonwealth Savings Bank book balance and it was only $85. That was short $45 and I still had to pay accommodation in Brisbane and then would need money for extras. *Hell, what was I to do?* I had already committed myself to the job.

"What's wrong Jack? You look rather sick. Are you alright?" said Mrs Thompson.

"Well, you know I applied for a job at Julia Creek and was successful, but the fares alone will cost me $130 and all the money I've got is $85. Seems I will have to break my word and ruin my name."

"When do you have to pay up?"

"This afternoon, so the agent can book and pay for my fare. What am I going to do?"

"Jack, I think I might be able to help you out to cover some of your costs, if that would help?"

"I can't borrow or take your money; I must try and manage things myself."

"There are times in life that we all need a helping hand and this is the time for you," said Mrs Thompson, "I will lend you what you need and the boys will take up a collection for you tonight. It's obvious you need the fare, so if you can wait a few minutes, I will see what I can do."

The dear, dear lady came back with $70.

"Will this help out?"

"Bless you, Mrs Thompson," I replied, "I promise to pay you back with my first pay check."

"I know you will, Jack, but you better get to the bank before it closes and pay the agent before it's too late."

"Thank you again Mrs Thompson," I said as I hurried out the door on my way, with passbook in hand to withdraw $60, leaving me $25 in my bank account and a big debt.

Off to the agent's office, then I gave the huge sum of money to Mrs Gillespie who then handed me all my travel documents and tickets. Thanking her for her great help in my time of need, I skipped out of the office and headed back to the boarding house to start packing.

That night after dinner, as I was finalising the packing of my meagre belongings, Tom walked in and said, "You off to Northen Queensland, are you? I hear you have a job as a stockman. I thought you were hanging out to go shearing."

"As you know, Tom," I replied, "the sheds haven't started yet and I need a good paying job, so I jumped in and took this one, but I didn't have enough for the fare and Mrs Thompson lent me $70 to get me by. But I feel awful taking it."

"Do you now?" said Tom, "Well I'm going to make things a bit better. We all have taken a collection up for you tonight of $28."

"Gee, thanks so much but I already owe $70. I can't take any more."

"Jack, take the money. Treat it as a gift. One of us will be short sometime and then we might claim it back." Then Tom just turned around and walked out without a further word.

At breakfast I thanked all the boarders for their donation to me. They all looked a bit embarrassed. (If you do something good for someone then do it, no good going on about it.)

I said, "See ya," to everyone and thanks, then gave a hug to Mrs Thompson, which was the only way I knew how to give a special thanks, then I was off with my gear to catch the Skinners bus for Brisbane.

The bus was half empty, so I had the two seats to myself. Spreading out and relaxing, I watched the passing scenery. It was rural country. Tall gum trees lined the road but now and then I spied sheep and cattle laying or standing in the paddocks' shady trees, but there was always a few stock still grazing out in the hot sun. A heat haze was bouncing off the road and my shirt felt damp as it was sticking to the bus's vinyl seat. With the window slightly ajar, I felt the warm breeze giving a very slight cooling effect.

A few hours later, we came to a large town called Warwick, with a few historic stone churches and their large steeples. A long main street dissected the town and this was where the bus made a comfort stop, as well as picked up more passengers.

I spread out my gear over the two seats hoping any newcomers wouldn't park themselves beside me. I left the bus for a toilet break and bought a Cottee's orange to drink as I was feeling thirsty and we still had a long way to go to Brisbane. I should have bought some sandwiches, but time was something I didn't have, as the bus driver beeped his horn, indicating it was time to board the bus to continue the journey. New passengers started to fill the bus but thank goodness my two seats were unoccupied.

The country was more open now with ploughed paddocks and some with young crops after recent showers. The further we went, there were smaller blocks of land and the occasional farmhouse was seen, with more cars on the road. With more people on the bus, I could catch bits of conversation.

Most of the passengers were well dressed. The men wore white shirts and ties, some with suits or sports jackets, even in this hot weather. But they all had hats: some felt, others straw, some cotton, but all with good brims for shading the head from the hot sun. The ladies were well dressed in pretty coloured dresses. An odd one or two had woollen suits on, with skirts well below the knee, but again, they all had hats, some felt, but most raffia, with decorations on them. Still with very wide brims. There were a couple of workers like me with cotton trousers, opened neck shirts, boots or riding boots. They were expensive, so most working blokes had only one pair of footwear. What I could gather, most of my travelling companions were going shopping, to a specialist, a funeral, a wedding, or just catching up with relatives. Then there was me, travelling to a new position.

Seeing a range of mountains ahead, we started climbing,

leaving the flat, undulating, farming country, which I learnt was called the Darling Downs. We were now moving from farming land into forest country. The bus was changing gears as we climbed steeper and steeper. I heard someone say we were going over Cunninghams Gap, whatever that meant. The bus was climbing into the lower gears and stayed there as we started to go down a very narrow, steep, curvy road. A few passengers were hanging on to the seat rails in front of them and, to be very honest, I wasn't a very happy soul, as the bus lurched from side to side. From my window, I could see miles below. If we went over the side, which was possible, we would all be killed. It was, in fact, a very dangerous road to be travelling on.

Much to everyone's relief, we arrived alive at a tiny town called Aratula, for a much-needed comfort stop. This was obvious as there was a rush to get out of the bus and quickly walk to the conveniences.

The further northeast we went, more farmland, then houses appeared and more cars: Holdens, Fords, a couple of Japanese cars and a few old jalopies and the occasional English motorbike went roaring past. We came to a big city, which I thought was Brisbane, but our driver said it was Ipswich. A stop to let off some passengers and a couple came on board. it wasn't long before suburbs came into view. I think I must have dozed off as it was farms one minute and next minute, it was all houses and factories and service stations.

We arrived at the Queensland Tourist Bureau in Queen Street, where we all tumbled out of the bus with our belongings, heading in our various destinations. I had quite a long walk up Queen Street to the Astoria Hotel, with my large backpack, airways bag in one hand and another bag in my other. There were a few rests on the way. I was surprised how much extra gear I had accumulated. Arriving well after 3pm, I booked a room overlooking the Brisbane River, then, taking my boots off,

I decide to have a camp, as the bus trip and the long walk with all my gear was enough for this young fella.

That evening, I rang Joan, my special girlfriend. We had discussed earlier about me wanting to make enough money and a 12-month separation before we finally decided to get married. She was delighted to hear from me. We talked and natted and then I gave her the news.

"Guess what, I'm going to Julia Creek as a stockman and the money is nearly three times I was earning as a jackaroo. I'm leaving on my first aeroplane this Friday morning."

"That's excellent for you, but I wish you wouldn't," she said, "I would prefer if you stayed here with me, Dad could find you a good job and anyway, I had told you money wasn't a concern, but I know your mind is made up.

"Anyhow, I have a surprise for you. I will be in Brisbane tomorrow and we can meet and be together again. May I suggest we meet in Queen Street at the Queensland Tourist Bureau, say 11.30 and then we can have lunch together."

"Oh Joan, that will be great," I replied, "See you at 11.30 then my love. Gotta go, the telephone is running out of coins. Bye darling."

I did want to see her again, truly, but the heart ache leaving her at Lota Station: the emotion, tears, last hugs and kisses, was all too much for me. Now I will have to go through it all again. Oh dear. I suppose it will be worth it, I hope so. I might get lucky, like in the Second World War, when soldiers were leaving for overseas engagements and they told their girls they could be killed and would they relent from their high moral code and give a 'bit' instead of waiting for marriage? Suppose it's not the same just going to Julia Creek, but...?

Next morning, I showered and shaved and put on clean underpants and even ironed a shirt. My feelings were mixed, one of excitement to see her again and another of dread. As I practically skipped down Queen Street to meet my love, I was early and so was she a few minutes later. It was great to see her; she looked heavenly. My heart skipped two beats. How could I leave an angel like this? I must be mad.

We hugged and kissed, held hands and walked down the street feeling a togetherness. We looked at shop windows, checking out our likes and dislikes and I managed, very skilfully, to divert her attention, as we walked past jewellery shops. We stopped at the picture theatre where they were advertising "To Kill a Mockingbird" and "Cleopatra" and the one I wanted to see, which was "The Magnificent Seven".

Unfortunately, Joan had to leave to go back to Lota at 1.30, giving us limited time together, so we found a very posh café in the arcade and just ordered mixed sandwiches for two and a pot of tea, thank you. We talked about everything and nothing. She enquired about my new job, not very enthusiastically, I must admit. I asked her about what was going on at Lota and her dad's property. But our future, the kids we were going to have, where we would marry and live had been discussed before and we both felt it just wasn't the best time now.

Joan asked the waitress if she could use the phone and she replied, yes, she could.

"This way madam."

Joan excused herself, left me wondering why she wanted to use the phone. I soon found out. Her mum was at their accountants and she was letting her know where to meet us. Well, that put an end to the soldier's plan of asking the sweetheart for extra love before going overseas.

Not long after, Joan's mother, Mrs Fisher, found us and shared another pot of tea. She asked what I was going to do. I gave a brief run down as I did not know much myself. Then she said, "We are all sad you are leaving us Jack, but Mr Fisher thinks it would be good for both of you to have a bit of a break before a lifetime commitment. Joan and I don't necessarily agree with Mr Fisher, do we darling? I'll just finish this cuppa and you two find a quiet spot to say your goodbyes."

We found a little alcove nearby; we held each other tightly. We kissed and I tasted her salty tears. I said time would go quickly.

"I do love you so, I will write." I then turned away from this beautiful woman and walked out of the arcade without looking back, a single tear sliding down my cheek.

I was excited going on a big jet, wow, at the Eagle Farm Airport. I watched big planes, small planes, landing and taking off and I was going in one. Clutching the ticket in my sweaty hand, I started to walk onto the airfield, the smell of jet fuel and other strange aromas ascended into my nostrils. My fellow passengers, smartly dressed in suits and felt hats, carrying their leather briefcases by the handles. There were a few smartly dressed women, but they were in the minority. They all accompanied me as I was climbing the stairs into the aircraft.

I started to get a bit worried, being a bit claustrophobic. I thought they were going to lock me into a tin container and thrust me into the atmosphere, but I was committed. Like riding a young horse, you just had to squash feelings and get on with the job.

But maybe there could be a reason I was apprehensive, for in the back of my mind, I remembered when I was eight years old and my father, who was separated from my mother, took me on a visit to Moorabbin Airport and shouted me a Ten Bob joy flight. I think it was in an Austa light plane. A pilot in the single front seat and two passengers in the back seat. I remember my father grabbing me by the hand and approaching the little plane and asking the pilot, was there any room for the little one? The pilot looked back at his two strapped in passengers and asked if they minded. They didn't, but there was no seat for me, so I was told to stand behind the pilot's seat and hang on tightly to the back.

Throttling up for take-off, the aircraft shook and rattled, then we were in the air. I couldn't see much as the pilot's back blocked my view, but I could just see a bit of blue sky out of the window. The pilot asked the passengers where they wanted to go and they said a scenic flight along the coastline. The little aircraft banked sharply to the left without warning. I have really just summarised at this point of the story, as I really don't recollect the little details of it all, but I do remember, as if it was yesterday, when the pilot banked that aircraft.

The sudden movement made me lose my grip of the seat and I fell over and banged against the pilot's door which flew open. Then I had my first view of the ground from 1000 feet.

My legs were grabbed by a passenger who hastily pulled me back into the plane. The pilot then closed the door and held onto it for the rest of the flight. He asked me if I was alright. I said, yes, and then he mentioned to the passengers that there was no need to say anything and that he was returning to the airfield and there was no charge for this flight. So, you're lucky that I'm still here to write this tale.

There was another incident when I was five years old, which I will tell you about later. It was about a steam train and a fire.

Back in the jet with seat belt on tight, a gentleman, sitting next to me in the window seat, was a bit different from the other passengers. He was young but older than me, dressed in a colourful open neck shirt, lite cotton slacks and brown shoes with tassels on them. We introduced ourselves: me, Jack and he, Miles, I proudly I told him I was on my way to Julia Creek with a new job as a stockman. Miles suggested I forget that and instead, travel the world. It was the best for a young man to see how other people lived and be educated on the history and geography of different countries. I thought, it was alright for him in his fancy clothes and tasselled shoes. Gosh, I had to borrow money just to get to Julia Creek. How in the hell was I going to travel the world?

He was a nice chap, telling me where he had been and was going to Cairns to catch a flight to New Guinea. The attractive hostess came with tea and sandwiches, which we enjoyed in silence and soon we had to prepare to land. I think it was Rockhampton. Taking off again after a short break, the next stop was Townsville where I had to catch another aircraft to Julia Creek.

Miles and I had run out of conversation. He looked out of the window while I had a nap as it was a long and eventful day. Fastening our seat belts, Miles gave me a nudge.

"We're landing in Townsville, so I wish you all the luck in your new job, but you should still think about going abroad."

I returned the good wishes as we bumped along the landing strip towards the terminal which was just a small building amongst other larger buildings which, I guess, were hangers and workshops. I noticed a few small planes, as well as jets, as we walked to the terminal.

A pie and tea, a walk, checking out other passengers, different dress codes and hats, you could tell the bushman from the businessman to the casual holiday makers and again a few ladies in their finery, but kids seemed to be missing. Probably all too expensive to fly. We boarded a Fokker Friendship aircraft on its way to Mt Isa. Julia Creek was about halfway.

It was a bumpy trip with the aircraft hitting a lot of air pockets. The hostess said it was normal for this flight in summer. I think we did six landings altogether. That's from Brisbane to Julia Creek and it was this landing I didn't want. From the window, the country was flat and looked very dry. The airfield was an airstrip and nothing else.

Was I supposed to get off here? No one else was getting

off. That's not good. The hostess opened the aircraft door. I walked out of the air-conditioned plane to hell on earth. The heat knocked me back; it really was like walking into an oven. Or was it the flies that knocked me back? It wasn't a few or 10, but hundreds and thousands. They were moisture-holics. They went for the eyes, nose and mouth, the ears. Even worse, they could crawl in or out of every orifice. I desperately tried to get back into the plane. I think I was given a nudge and the aircraft door shut. Guess they didn't want the flies.

I walked down the ramp, carrying my hand luggage and a tonne of crawling flies. A car, or was it a taxi, was waiting for me not that far from the aircraft. A man came from behind the plane with my gear.

"You Jack, here is your luggage. Now, let's get you into town."

The FJ Holden had all windows open; it was hot as hades to match the hell on earth. I climbed into the hot seat,

"Gannon's Hotel good enough for you son?"

"Yeah, that would be fine. Geez, it's bloody hot and the flies! How the heck do you live here?"

"You get used to it, but you did have to come here in the heat of summer with a bad drought in progress. The flies, they go when the sun goes down."

"Yeah, but I bet they are there when the sun comes up."

"Yer right there, but you will soon learn the Aussie wave," said my driver, "By the way, my name's Robert and welcome to the Creek."

"Yeah thanks," I replied. "I have a stockman's job with Lindfield Station."

"Oh, the Sailen brothers," he nodded, "They're all right, there are much worse places to work than at Lindfield."

We arrived at our destination, a dusty shimmering small town in a hot, hostile, open plain country. The last place I wanted to be. We stopped at the pub.

The pub was busy. It was just after 6pm. In Melbourne, they would be closing the hotel doors at six but here in Queensland, as long as you were 21 years of age you could drink from 10am to 10pm or in small towns, sometimes the local police and publican decided.

The flies were slowly diminishing, as was the sun. I thought I better wait for my new boss outside, even though I could have done with a cold drink. A few blue singlet men passed me on the way going into the pub and giving me the once over. Nothing said, just a nod in my direction. There were a couple of dark people about. They weren't Aborigines, just very dark, even a gun metal blue. Big, strong, tall, muscled men which I found out later were Thursday Islanders who were working on a new beef railway line. Evidently, it was too hot a job up here for whites or Aborigines, so they brought the tough, good men from the islands to do the work.

A blue zephyr car pulled up and a fit-looking man, about my size, about 30, got out and said, "You Jack Alexander?" I said I was. "I'm Barry Sailen, manager of Lindfield station. Put your gear in the boot and get in the back, we're running a bit late." Then he got back in the car. I stuffed, yes stuffed, my gear into the boot then stuffed myself into the back seat, which also was full of parcels and boxes.

Barry turned around and introduced his wife, who was sitting next to him.

"This is my wife, Emma. This is Jack our new stockman."

This attractive woman gave me a smile and said, "Welcome Jack. I hope you are going to like it here at Lindfield."

I said, "I hope so too."

She had a fashionable hat on and was extremely well dressed. I would dare to say a bit too much for this kind of environment, but when you're in the bush, especially the ladies, really like to dress up going to town or visiting. They didn't go out much, so it was always a special occasion.

The couple talked between themselves; I couldn't hear much in the back with the rumble of the black dirt road we were travelling on. I gathered from snatches of conversation, they had been visiting friends or family and shopping, talking about the day's events.

We were travelling northeast on a rough black soil road. I think we travelled 35 kilometres and then turned off for Lindfield, another eight kilometres. The sun was starting to set; the country was flat but there were tall gum trees along the road and nowhere else.

Tired and cramped, at last we arrived at the station. It was a white, typical Queensland homestead, with two attached buildings. One, I guessed was the kitchen. I helped unload the car and then Barry pointed to the quarters and said, "You should find a room there."

Carrying my gear, I opened the homestead's little back gate, crossed the little wooden bridge, which was over a bore drain, and walked to my quarters, a partly gauzed, iron building, with a bit of a veranda. Noticing two empty rooms, divided completely by corrugated iron sheets, I chose the southern one.

The furniture: a wooden kitchen table with a chair to match, one old three ply wardrobe with two drawers and a wooden single bed with wire base and a mattress which I guessed was filled with coconut husk or some other stuffing. Folded at the end of the bed was a dusty grey army blanket. Oh dear, I didn't think. I wasn't a jackaroo anymore, supplied with nice rooms, good bed, linen, blankets and pillows. As a jackaroo, I was in the upper-class bracket; as a stockman I was in the lower-class.

Toilets? You ask. There wasn't one. Bathroom? There wasn't one. But there was a little shed attached with some concrete washing troughs. There was also a surprise - hot and cold water, would you believe? It was discovered later, at the homestead, there was a hot flowing bore where the windmill filled the big high tank, then two outlets: one was cold, (never cold, warm), the other went down through the hot bore drain and delivered hot water to the homestead and to the quarters, after tracking 200 feet. A bell rang. I guessed it was teatime. No time to change but didn't matter now I was a stockman. A quick wash and a brush of the hair and off to the men's dining room.

I walked up three steps and opened the squeaky screen door into a small, painted, white room with a wooden table and four wooden chairs. The table was set with a green plastic tablecloth in the centre, the salt and pepper, sauce bottles, jam, a small jug of milk covered by a cloth with beads and a glass container with a lid held the margarine. I chose the chair at the head of the table, thinking it might give me an air of authority. Sitting down, I noticed, to my right, an open doorway I guessed went into the kitchen. The aromas from the kitchen did not get my digestive juices going wild.

Then another figure opened the fly screen door. As he stepped in, he looked at me and introduced himself.

"I'm Bob, the cowboy." (If I may explain, a cowboy on a Queensland station is not like the cowboys in western movies. A cowboy here does the station jobs, such as milking, killing the station meat, looking after and feeding the chooks and pigs. Tending the vegetable garden and gardens generally, plus watering and mowing lawns etc.)

I stood up, shook his hand and said, "I'm Jack, the new stockman."

His hand felt like a cold, wet fish. (Yuck, I self-consciously wiped my hand on to my trousers). He didn't seem the most intelligent sort of chap. But then one mustn't go on looks alone. He had a pale complexion, fair hair and very light blue eyes. Tall, thin as a rake with spidery fair hair on his face and arms.

Our meal arrived, carried by a plump girl I guessed was in her early 20s. As she placed my dinner in front of me, she informed me her name was Susan, the station cook. I said, "I'm Jack, the new stockman."

Going by her accent I asked, "Are you a Pommy?"

She replied, yes, she was from Leicestershire and was doing a 12-month stint in Australia. As she disappeared into the kitchen, Bob said under his breath, "She aint no cook."

I had to agree, after eating my meal of mutton stew with peas, carrots and mashed potatoes. Conversation was nil as we chewed and swallowed the meal without much pleasure. Sweets were brought in - junket and stewed apricot - plates taken away and a pot of tea brought in. As I poured the tea, I asked Bob where he stayed. He told me there were other quarters like mine a few 100 feet away. He said they were bloody awful and they were going to be pulled down and a new one was to be built.

"But I have been here six months and so far, nothing has happened and probably won't."

"Bob, where is the dunny?"

"There isn't one, that's got to be built too. Go down to the bore drain near the horse yards and you can shit there. I'll show you around tomorrow after my chores if you like,"

"What do I do for toilet paper?"

"Ask the boss, he will give you a roll." Then Bob just jumped up and left by the screen door. I followed after finishing my tea and smoke.

I found my way to the quarters, tired after a long day and again wondering, what have I got myself in for? I should have come with my torch; it was dangerous in snake country to walk in the dark without a light, but I managed to get to my bed without being bitten. I just flopped on the bed, no unpacking, no toothbrush, just sleep and more sleep. Glad I don't have to get up at 5:30 in the morning to run the horses in or do the chores. It went black as my eyes closed and it wasn't till the bloody flies woke me up with the sun the next morning that I surfaced. I got up, dressed into working clothes, washed, cleaned my teeth, brushed my hair and went to find Bob the cowboy to get some information.

At 6.15am, the sun was well up and starting to heat the day. The flies, being rested overnight, started to do their moisture gathering on my body. But not too bad yet, a wave every four seconds would do for now.

I noticed another quarters like mine and walked over, hoping to find Bob there. Hearing country and western music, I yelled, "You there, Bob?"

"What the hell are you doing waking people up at this hour?" a voice responded.

"Sorry mate, thought you were awake hearing Slim Dusty singing on the radio."

"Well, you can piss off. It's Saturday and breakfast isn't till 7.30."

"Sorry," and I slinked away and started to do some exploring.

I noticed, not far away, a house and guessed it was a married quarters, possibly where Barry's brother lived. But I turned in the other direction and walked to a line of mimosa bushes. Not far away, I glimpsed the horse yards.

I had to find where Bob said the so-called toilet was, but I had to suck it up till I had some paper. Oh, deary me. I found the toilet, as I walked in the line of bushes, there were dried-up turds, sorry, human faeces. Someone had done one there, someone else had a dump further down the line and so it went on. I think, with the extreme heat here in the summer, sometimes over 100 degrees, the human droppings cooked very quickly, so the flies preferred human faces instead of the turds.

Walking the extra 50 yards or so were the horse yards which were large, but no horses in sight. I turned round slowly. Walking towards the homestead, there were scattered bushes around the yards and homestead, but looking in the near distance was nothing, absolutely nothing. Just plain, open big country.

The bell rang, so I made my way to the kitchen. There was a box of Kellogg's corn flakes, a box of Weet-Bix and a big jug of milk on the table, as well as a jar of jam and vegemite. The other condiments were still there from the night before. I sat down and grabbed three Weetbix into the supplied china bowl, pouring in the mixed Sunshine powdered milk.

Bob walked in, said a gruff hello and sat down and grabbed the cornflakes.

"Don't you milk a cow?" I asked.

He didn't look up, but said, "I don't milk."

Guess he wasn't a morning person. Susan walked in, saying good morning with a smile. I returned both to her. She asked, "How many chops do you want?"

"Two thanks and do we get toast?"

"Yes, I'm doing the toast and the chops now; you'll just have to wait."

"I don't mind waiting, if you're the one bringing them in," I said with a cheeky smile.

I got a smile as she turned towards the kitchen. You gotta flirt a bit with the cook, your stomach relies on it. Bob, with his head still down, said, "Can I have four chops and forget about the toast?" as she returned to the kitchen.

After eating his breakfast in a hurry, Bob just left. I waited, leisurely drinking my tea and making the makings. I wanted to see Barry, the boss, and find out some details of what he wanted me to do, about the property and terms of employment.

It wasn't long before Barry came in with a mug of tea and sitting down, he said, "I'm sorry Jack, I haven't had a chance to talk to you or explain what's going on. Lindfield is a 200 square mile property, containing two other properties. One is called Losborn, the other Farlee. Farlee is our cattle place, run by big Peter with 800 head of cattle. Lindfield is running 40,000 sheep.

"As you may have guessed, we are in a severe drought and

we have no feed on Lindfield. We are taking the sheep on the road to drove them until it rains. That's where you come in, Jack. Have you had to drive sheep?"

"No, I haven't," I replied, "but I have worked a lot of sheep and done a day or two of moving them down the road for quite a few kilometres, so I feel I can handle what you have in mind."

"That's good," Barry said, "now we have mustered 6000 weaner and maiden ewes and they are in a holding paddock at Argyle station, which is next door.

"You, Len and Colin, they're both with the sheep now, will be driving them from Argyle station to Kynuna and if it doesn't rain by then, we'll keep heading south. We have a truck with all the food, gear, etc and are waiting for the cook, who we hope will be here on Sunday. We will pick you up early Monday morning.

"Have your swag and gear ready and I will tell you Sunday night the exact time I want you ready. In the meantime, get yourself familiar with the area and what gear you leave behind will be held in the storeroom, any questions?"

"Yes, who will be in charge of the drive?" I asked.

"Reg, my younger brother will start you off," Barry said, "but I will need him to help me later on, as I will be driving the rest of the sheep a couple of days behind you."

"Barry, I haven't got a saddle, bridle, saddle bag or quart pot."

"Go down to the saddle shed and pick what gear you need and put it with your stuff ready for pick up. I must go now, might see you during the weekend. Lunch is 12.30, dinner at 6:30, no smoko during the weekend."

"Oh, I nearly forgot, can I have some toilet paper?"

Barry walked off, then turned around and said, "Ask Susan."

I went into the kitchen and called for Susan. She soon came from somewhere or other.

"Susan, could you please get me some toilet paper."

"Just a minute, Jack, I will get you a roll, but it is precious, look after it." She came back with a large roll of cheap corrugated looking paper. Better than twigs or leaves for a wipe. "It's disgusting, you boys must go down to the mimosa bushes."

"Oh, so you don't have go there yourself?"

"No, silly. There's a septic toilet here in the house, but I must share it with the boss and his missus. The place is terribly rundown and in ill-repair. I think it was bought cheap and the boss has to improve it and get it properly operational again. He has just built a new 12 stand shearing shed and redone the shearers quarters, but with this drought, everything has come to a standstill. I gotta go, so see you at lunch, it will be just sandwiches. See ya,'" and she was gone.

I went straight to find the saddle shed for my gear. If I was to be on a horse all day every day, I wanted to get the best. There were large saddles, saddles with Mickey Mouse ears, (large knee pads), some with high cantles, (back of the seat that would break your back), and some with a high pommel, (front of the saddle, one could end up giving you a squeaky voice). I picked a nice Poley saddle, just slightly bigger in the seat, but it would suit me. I found a good bridle with red leather reins; a saddle bag and quart pot were already attached to the saddle. I spent the whole morning oiling and greasing all the leather gear till it was soft and supple.

After lunch, I unpacked and sorted all my gear, what to take and what to leave behind. First, I hand washed the old army blanket folded on my bed. I sorted all my belongings on the bed. I had a type a swag. It was just a large square of heavy brown duck, a tartan picnic rug with tassels on each end, my cotton single mattress cover and two accidentally acquired pillowcases. I packed two pairs of trousers, three shirts, three pair of socks, four large handkerchiefs, one pair of pyjama shorts, that were all rolled in a cheap plastic raincoat, shoving it all into one of the pillowcases.

The other pillowcase would hold toilet bag, towel, torch, book, wallet that had a few dollars, spare tins of tobacco and papers and the toilet paper. I rolled it all into the canvas and tied it up with two large red hide thongs, which could be used to repair broken leather gear or a whip fall. I would wear my hat, high heel tan riding boots, blue shirt and grey moleskin trousers, two large handkerchiefs, one to go round my neck and a spare, my stockman belt with attached stockman's knife in a leather pouch, a Smith's pocket watch in leather pouch and another leather pouch holding a tin of matches and, of course, my good kangaroo hide platted six-foot whip. It was what every good stockman carried while on his horse. Which brings me to the stockman's rule:- *Don't ever touch a stockman's dog, horse, saddle and gear, his hat, quart pot, saddle bag, stockman knife, watch and swag. These are all survival items.* There is not, in the stockman's rule, anything about a stockman's wife.

I must again mention the flies. They were consistently covering the whole of my back and face, driving me mad. I was waving them away and keeping my mouth tightly shut which, if anyone knows me, it's a very difficult thing for me to do. To prove how hot it was, the blanket I hand washed an hour ago, was completely dry. All right, if you want to get personal, I do not wear underpants unless I go to town.

The rest of the day, I had a bit of a look around and then had a camp till the bell rang for tea.

The next day was Sunday, the day of rest. I had my first bludge for ages. I read my book, 'These were my Tribesmen' by Allan Marshall. I checked all my gear ready for tomorrow and what I was putting in the storeroom. I wrote a letter to Joan and my mum. I wished I had some carbon paper as I could copy both letters as I said the same thing, except for an extra page to Joan with things my mum didn't need to know. Both letters said I did not know when I could send or receive letters as I was going droving with sheep to Kynuna and had no idea for how long, or when and how the next mailing would be. I was looking forward to the adventure, except for the heat and flies.

After lunch, walking back to my lavish quarters, I met a man, who was tall, smartly dressed in clean and pressed riding clothes, and yes, the highly polished tan high heeled Williams riding boots with spurs attached.

"You Jack? I'm Reg, the overseer, Barry's brother."

"Yea, I believe you and me and a couple of other blokes are going to drove sheep to Kynuna."

"Yes, that's right. I hope you're an experienced man with sheep because it will be a difficult drive for a few days. Did Barry tell you they are all weaners and maiden ewes?"

"Yes, he did and I'm keen to go, but I haven't seen or tried my horses out, where are they?"

"The horse team is yarded at Argyle Station. You will get used to the three horses assigned to you on the trip. We will have plenty of time to get to know each other. But I can't yarn now as I still have a lot of preparation to do getting ready for the drive."

C.2

Droving, Floods, Rescue

Breakfast, 6am. I put my swag in the Holden ute, with the rest of my gear into the storeroom. Breakfast menu was the same: cereal, chops, fried eggs, toast, mug of tea, then into the ute to Argyle Station.

I saw the sheep before I saw the homestead. I had never seen 6,000 sheep before, held together in one mob. A couple of chaps were shepherding them, while the sheep were looking for the sparse feed. We pulled up at some horse yards. I thought, *I'm the last to get my horses so I bet they will be the worst of the string.* There were three in the round yard. Barry said, "They're your three. Pick one out and saddle up and ride out to the sheep."

"Can I have time to ride all three?" I asked.

"No, you can't. We haven't got the time. Just saddle one and get to the mob as soon as you can."

I chose the smaller of the three, a 14 1/2 hand dappled blue mare. She seemed very apprehensive as I approached with bridle in hand. I took my time talking soothingly to her. As soon as I noticed she was accepting me, I slowly raised my hand to her near side neck. I gently put the reins around her neck, still talking, telling her what a beautiful girl she was. Then with the back of my hand over the head strap of the bridle gently rubbing her nose until I got the headstall on, I teased her mouth open so she would accept the bit.

I was a strange human to her and she was a strange horse to me. To get along together we had to move slowly, talking a lot till we accepted each other. Then the saddle blanket and saddle. She tensed up a bit as I buckled up the girth. I led her to the big yard, walked her round a few times then tightened the girth once more. A little walk then I quickly mounted, easing myself into the saddle. She humped a bit, but with me rubbing her mane and talking gently, she soon started to walk out freely.

A few more rounds of the yards, then I dismounted and had a quick look at my other two mounts, both bay geldings, a good 15 hands and looking fit and lean. I thought they might give me an experience but for now I remounted my horse, after closing the yard gate. She did a few crow hops but a talk and a rub and we were trotting towards the large mob of sheep.

I hadn't noticed until now, but the blue sky at breakfast had quite a few clouds, as if something was building up. Riding around the sheep, I saw what I thought was a kid on a grey gelding of about 16 hands.

"G'day I'm Jack, the new man, are you coming on the drive?"

"Yep, my name is Len and this is my second driving trip in three months," he replied, "How did you manage that horse? You know, she has thrown a few, even Colin over there on the wing. Did she buck much?"

"No, just a few crow hops," I said, pleased at his questions.

"Gee, you must be good or know something, but I just think you were lucky," he laughed.

"I'll see you later, I better go and see Colin. The sheep aren't moving much," I replied.

I came across the other stockman for this trip.

"You Colin? I'm Jack." I introduced myself.

"G'day, they told me someone else was coming to help with the drive. Is that you?" he said.

"Yep, but I dunno, I think by the look at the sky we might get a shower or two."

"Yes, but not enough to stop the drive. As you can see, no feed and we need inches to get the country healthy again. Did Lucy give you much trouble?"

"You mean the horse? Is that her name, Lucy?" I chuckled.

"Yes, but there is not many she will let on her back. She must like you."

"Oh, there is a couple of spots of rain. I'm surprised the sheep aren't feeding."

"It's getting too hot," said Colin, "They won't move in the heat, they just baulk, but with this bit of cloud cover and a few spots we might get our eight mile in today."

A heavy rain shower drenched us and the sheep. Seeing the sheep were staying still, I trotted up to a bower shed where Barry, Reg and the owner of Argyle, Ray Hicks, were drinking tea and having some sandwiches.

"Hey Jack, get yourself something to eat and drink, then go and relieve one of the boys for a break. We will get moving within the hour," said Barry.

I ate my corn beef and pickle sandwich, swallowed a mug of warm tea and trotted off to a wet Len and said, "Go up, get yourself a sandwich, then give Colin a break. The boss reckons we can start moving the sheep on the road in the hour."

"Yeah, that's right," said Len, "the rain is easing."

Then he cantered off to the shelter. The sheep were starting to get restless after the rain, some chasing a bit of dry feed while others just laid where they were.

Soon the drive was on. Reg took the lead, Colin and Len rode the wings in a clockwise and anticlockwise motion, passing me on their way to the other side of the sheep and I, being the new chap, was in the drag, pushing lagging sheep up and copping all the dust from 24,000 hooves.

The rain had stopped and, yippee, the flies started again. Will I ever get used to them crawling in to all my facial crevices? One hand on the reins and the other holding my whip, I was not very successful swatting the little moistureholics.

The sun decided to put on more heat before closing for the evening. I mentioned the dust, did I tell you it was competing with the flies, in my mouth, eyes and nostrils? If I blew my nose, mud would be on my hankie.

I have heard people say, "Oh, droving must be a romantic adventure."

Don't know where they get that idea from. Within a few hours, we arrived at Argyle station's boundary on the Nelia and Julia Creek Road junction.

A small body truck was there and a bloke was just finishing off putting in steel posts and running ringlock wire, attaching it to the boundary fence for the sheep break that night. We ringed the sheep, (stockman are quite often called ringers), until one ewe led all the others in. When the makeshift gate closed on the sheep, Reg said, "I didn't think it was that easy to drive 6,000 sheep and pen them all without any trouble."

Colin whispered, to no one in particular, "The sheep are poor and hungry, wait till they get some nutritional food into them. I bet we won't have it too easy from now on."

The man with the truck, who had put the break up, was our new cook, called Dick. After the second day, we called him Dick the Flick as he never wore footwear. As he prepared camp meals, bits of mud and dirt from between his toes would flick into the cooking or, I'm sure, on our dinner plates. He got the sack a couple of days later as he was a bad and dirty cook.

After the sheep had settled down, I unsaddled Lucy and

brushed her down, then I started the mammoth job of untangling her mane and tail, which was all matted and knotted from lack of care. I do like to ride a groomed lady. Hobbles, or tethers, on, she joined the others feeding on dry oaten hay. A few bales of the stuff were kept in the front of the truck and on top of the covered stock crate. A yarn and smoke as we squatted watching our meal being prepared of freshly killed steak (last we would get as from then on it was salted dry meat), boiled potatoes and beans, plus a slice of bread and jam and, as always, mugs of hot tea.

Colin and I, after our meal, went to check on the horses, to make sure they had not wandered too far. Seeing we had horse bells on them, it wasn't required, as we heard the bells clanging all night. It was decided we would take it in turns to make sure the horses were ready in the morning for saddling.

Our first night under the stars. They were so close, I felt I could pluck them out of the sky. They lit up the country like if it was an early daylight. It was a magnificent sight. It is known you can muster stock on such a night. I just lay there in my swag looking up at an amazing creation. It was beautiful.

Reg said, before he took off with Barry in the ute back to Lindfield, that he wanted to start on the road by 5.45am. This meant we were to get up before five, have the horses in and saddled, have a quick breakfast and make our lunch.

Early at piccaninny daylight, I brought the 14 horses in with bells clanging as they trotted towards the hay that I had put out previously. Colin and Len caught and saddled their horses and saddled Reg's up as well. I picked Lucy again as she had not worked much the day before. Saddling her, she was a bit tense, but after a bit of a walk and talk she seemed to relax.

The cook did not help much. He was a bit tardy getting up and starting the fire. Len was on hand to help the lazy sod while Colin and I did everything else to get ready by the starting time.

Finishing our breakfast and making lunch, enjoying our mug of tea and first smoke for the day, Barry pulled up in the ute, dropping Reg off.

"Right boys, let's get mounted and get this mob on the road." Barry partly opened the break gate, while Colin, Len and I were ready to hold the lead as Reg started to count out the 6,000 sheep.

All hell broke loose. The weaner/maiden ewes came out of the break in a frenzied run, some leaping as Reg was trying to get an accurate count. The three of us had a hectic time trying to hold the mob in some sort of control. As the count went on, the sheep just spread in all directions looking for the elusive feed. By some miracle, we were able to keep them in some sort of order, but by the time Reg had finished the count, we were holding the mob three kilometres from the break. Now the proper droving began.

Every day from then on was the same. Flies, heat, dust and hard tack. Lips dry, prickle heat on the neck, dry mouth from lack of water and overall dehydrated. We started by daybreak as the sheep stopped, yes stopped, at about 10.30. It was the heat, you see; they just sat, an odd few stayed standing but did not move. You just couldn't move them and the council rule was 15k a day for sheep. The sheep started to move by three. So, there we were, from 10.30am to 2.30pm, give a minute or two, of four hours, standing in the heat of the middle of the day in the open downs. No shade except from what you can get from your horse, sometimes underneath till the horse changed his position.

We sometimes stood or squatted into pairs, giving each other a bit of shade. Flies, don't mention the flies. Our arms got tired of waving them from our face, so a large handkerchief was worn to keep a few off. Try eating your lunch. Give a quick wave, a quick bite of the dried-out sandwich and you would probably get three of four flies to flavour it. Yes, we had limited water, one of us would go to the truck for the canvas water bag to give everyone a drink. Not too much though, just a mouthful. A bit about drinking water later.

No sheep dogs? You say. Reg had one, but it was pretty useless. It was just too hot for working dogs.

Now it was not correct in saying every day was the same. There was one night and one day that was different. We had been driving sheep for three days in hot, humid conditions and no water for them as we would give them a drink at Julia Creek's creek. I think we were about three kilometres from the creek when the sheep started to pick up a bit of pace, which was surprising. The sheep increased their speed, we tried to slow them down.

Someone yelled, "They have smelt the water, hold them."

We tried; we tried damn hard. We cracked our stock whips, we yelled, we galloped back and forward to hold the lead. I had heard of cattle rushing or stampeding but never sheep and yet, that's what the blighters were doing. They went crazy for water. They ran under the horses, they banged into the horses' legs, the horses were confused as we, with this avalanche of 6,000 white sheep. There was nothing we could do. They ran on, over the backs of sheep that were drinking, as if they were a bridge, then continued over the other side into the town and into the common. It was mayhem, panic.

(I do have a print by Tom Roberts called the Break, it is so realistic as to what happened to us on that day.)

We spent the rest of the day gathering the sheep in the town and common. We managed, by sheer determination, to get the mob together and make all the sheep have a good drink. We held them on the creek till night fall, then drove them to the town's sale sheep yards. The towns people came from everywhere, watching the now calmed mob being driven to the yards. Photos were taken and some said it was the last of the big droves. Which it was.

Of the 6,000 sheep, we lost 11. Whether they were lost or hanging up slaughtered in some of the town's back yard sheds, we may never know. We were too tired to go to the pub, so had our cooked dinner, the last by Dick the Flick, as he wasn't wanted any more.

Day four, we counted out the sheep. That's how we knew we were eleven short. They were behaving well. The sheep behind must have thought the ones had better feed in front, so they passed them. It was like a rolling cloud. Surprisingly, they actually moved faster than driving cattle.

A bit of trouble, no names mentioned, but I was not involved, thank God. But one of the men came up and said to me, "Have you been pinchin' my peanuts?"

"No, and I didn't think we were allowed to have sweets or luxuries, and it was one of the stockman's rules never to touch another man's swag," I replied.

He said he would find the culprit out.

Three days later he said to me, "I found out who pinched me peanuts and I taught him a lesson."

"How did you do that?" I asked.

"I checked on yous, all after yous had a crap and found the one with peanuts in it. I dug them out and put them back in the empty packet and they were gone the next day. That will teach him."

Well, the drive went on. Our meals improved with the new cook, Cecil. He did a great job, seeing he had limited supply of bought stores and, with this heat, food went off quickly. Every day was the same as every day. Dust, flies, heat, the stink of sheep, sore bum, the prickly heat and this godforsaken country in the grip of a severe drought.

Laying on my swag, having a blissful sleep, I was woken up by a thunderous noise at midnight. *What's that?* I went to sleep under a blue sky. But it was thunder and streaks of lightning flashed. And then it rained, no, not a sprinkle but a tropical storm.

We were all sleeping under a lean-to tarp, which had one side attached to the side of the truck and the other end with a couple of poles. It collapsed under the heavy rain. We were soaked; we were dazed. Where did the rain come from? There was no warning. We tried to save our swags and other items from the constant sheets of water.

The cook yelled, "Let the sheep out of the break, or you will lose them."

But we were in some one's property. Were we allowed? How would we get them back? What to do?

"Don't muck about, get the sheep out NOW!" We opened the break and the sheep just bolted out under heavy rain into nowhere.

Later, it was found we had four inches of rain in three quarters of an hour. No sleep for the rest of the night as damp and wet gear needed to be dried out. At daylight, we checked the break, which was flattened on one side and there were hundreds of sheep bogged in the black soil mud. They had been run over by thousands of sheep in their panicked rush.

We took the cord girths off our saddles and, in pairs, we knelt in the mud and placed the girth under a sheep, after cleaning mud from its mouth, nostrils and eyes. Then, holding each end of the girth, we both, with a lot of effort, pulled the animal from the sucking black mud. Waited till it had its feet, before it staggered out to find its mates. It was hot, dirty tiring work, but out of the 150 sheep that were bogged, we managed to save 140. An excellent job done under shocking conditions.

Nothing to do for the rest of the day but dry our things, fix up the boggy mess of the camp and check on the horses. We were all so tired, so we had a good long camp. Reg rode back along the road to see how his brother, Barry, had managed the storm. They were two days behind us, bringing the rest of the Lindfield sheep.

Here we were, stuck in the middle of nowhere. That's me, Colin, Len and the cook. Our supplies and our diet, for the next three days, consisted of: Weetbix, tin peas, four loaves of mildewed bread, plus the most important things, tobacco and tea. We just couldn't live without them.

We cleaned up the camp, brushed the horses and cleaned our saddle gear. We slept and yarned and slept and yarned. The stories that were told were slightly exaggerated or just downright lies.

Reg came back on day three, mentioning that if we could move the truck back to Barry's camp, without getting bogged, we could help Barry with his mob to get back to Lindfield.

"Jack get your horse saddled and come with me."

We had to find the owner of the property where our sheep were running free. I asked Reg how long it took to find Barry and how many sheep did he lose? He told me it took six hours to reach him, slogging through the black, boggy mud. And he and his horse were exhausted after the slow hard ride. There were parts of the road he could get a bit of a trot up; others were covered in water and slow going. I also asked him when he thought the road would be all right to travel on. He did not think it would be for another day or two. I told him we had no tucker. He said he was working on it. Great. Anyhow, how many sheep did Barry lose? Reg, with a hint of a smile, said twice as many as us. He had left it too late to open the break.

After opening and closing a few gates, we eventually arrived as we rode our horses up to the homestead, a typical Queenslander with verandas all around and, I suspect, it had quite a pretty garden but now most of it had been smashed by the heavy rain.

"Hey there, anyone about?" yelled Reg in his loudest voice.

After the second yell, a small middle-aged man came out through the screen door putting on his large brim sweat-stained Akubra hat.

"What are you fellas after?"

Reg dismounted, handed me the reins of his horse and walked up to where the man stood. I heard them introduce themselves with a shake of the hand, then they moved to a couple of squatter chairs, where they apparently discussed the rain and letting 6,000 sheep run on his property. I was still left in the hot sun (don't forget the bloody flies). Not being able to hear their conversation, I dismounted and moved myself and the two horses under the shade of a couple of Athol pines nearby, rolled a smoke and waited. I thought if the missus brings out a tray of tea and scones to the two men, stuff the horses I was going to join them, but the event didn't occur.

After quite a while, Reg came back, we mounted and rode back to camp. Reg said that Mr Molloy was very understanding and said to leave the sheep till things dry out. He would come down on his tractor in the afternoon with some food from the station's storeroom.

Flour for damper, powdered milk, baking soda, six tins of baked beans, some salted meat, rice, tin peas and carrots. His wife cooked a huge swag of pikelets and we all hopped into them, which ended up making us feel a bit sick, after our meagre rations we had been on. So, a big thank you to Mr and Mrs Molloy and his big international tractor.

Mr Molloy suggested another day or two and the road should be passable for travelling. He would come down in his Land Rover four-wheel drive to check the road. If he could get through, he would take Reg back to Barry. And so, it was.

Reg left early with Mr Molloy, while the four of us waited to see what was going to happen. We pulled down the damaged break; it was difficult to roll up the muddy damaged ringlock wire. It was hot, humid, hard work. Then we tidied the truck and packed as much as we could, then checked on the horses, who had wandered off chasing the bit of green pick that started to show.

Later that afternoon, Mr Molloy arrived without Reg, so we guessed they made it to the other camp all right. With a note in his hand, Mr Molloy read out the instructions. The truck should be able to leave in the morning with Colin, Len and Cecil the cook.

"Jack, you are to stay behind and bring all the horses back to Lindfield," Mr Molloy read, "Reg said you will need food and enough drinking water for yourself for a few days. He also said, take all that you need and give the horses a good feed of hay tonight and in the morning."

Oh, Jack, I thought to myself, *you have got the short stick again. What's so special about me that I seem to get the difficult jobs.* Then another thought struck me, I was too busy watching and driving the sheep, being so new to this country, I wasn't sure where Lindfield Station was. All I really have to do is back track along this boring road to Julia Creek and, from then on, I hoped the horses could show me the way home.

After breakfast, they left me on my lonesome at six the next morning. The horses had their hay, I had damper, cooked rice, two packets of dates in my saddle bag and I had a lend of Len's saddle bag, tied to the off side of my saddle with my quart pot. In that bag was, cereal, powdered milk, one packet of sultanas and three oranges and two apples. All donated by Mr Molloy.

For water they left me a full canvas water bag. I fashioned it into a sort of harness. A neck strap and on the leather back of the canvas bag, I attached a leather strap to the girth. How successful it would be, time would tell. But there would be lots of muddy puddles for me and the horses on our way. I was loaded up with the rations and water, 13 horses plus my mount, with knee hobbles fastened around their necks. On the horses with the two bells, I put leather stoppers on the clappers. We were on the road by seven at a fair pace.

I thought I would catch up to the other camp, but I didn't. I found out later that where Barry had let the sheep go, he paid for agistment for them to stay there for six weeks and they all went home for comfort and cooked meals. Meanwhile, back on the road, me, Jack with the flies, burning sun, prickly heat and sore blistered bum. And the water bag with the ingenious made harness failed mid-morning and ended up on the road in an unworthy condition with all water lost. Don't worry about me, I had plenty of muddy contaminated water on the side of the road to drink.

The sun was sinking down in the horizon. It must be nearly 6pm. That's riding about 11 hours, including the 15 minutes or so rest every two hours for the horses and me. But where to camp, or do I ride to Julia Creek?

As providence would have it, there was a yard and loading ramp I spied just before dark. I put the horses in the yard, gave Ched, one of my bay geldings, a good strong horse that knew his job, a through rub down. Checked out a good place to sleep, there wasn't any. It was a smelly saddle blanket for a bed and a saddle for a pillow.

The horses and I were provided with an old trough, presumably filled by the recent rain. I scooped a quart pot full and looked around for some fuel to light a small fire. I ended up scraping wood off the yard rails with my stockman's knife and using other bits of fuel I found on the ground. I managed to boil the quart pot for the much-needed tea. A bit of damper, an orange, a hand full of dates. I was tired so that's all I needed.

I gazed into the flames and burning coals. I was transfixed by the fire, like another fire I was transfixed by. It was so long ago; I must have been four or five years old, just after World War

Two. It was at Spencer Street railway station and there was a huge steam engine with smoke billowing out of its smokestack. Steam was busy caressing the giant wheels and the thundering noise from this monster was awe inspiring to my small mind.

A friendly fireman said to my mum, leaning out of the huge engine, "Give me the little chap, all kids like to be in a steam locomotive."

My mother lifted me up to the fireman then, holding me, he opened the fire box door. I saw a red, hot, ferocious, devouring fire from hell. I screamed blue murder; I screamed like I had never screamed before. The kindly fireman passed me quickly back to my mother. They couldn't understand why I was so terrified when they asked me, but then I was not old enough to explain, that I thought the fireman was going to throw me into the fire. I must have heard a conversation about the holocaust and how people and children were thrown into furnaces. After those memories, the fire slowly burnt down and I went soundly to sleep.

Had a mug of tea and a weetbix with powdered milk and a bruised apple for breakfast, then I saddled up early for that day's ride. I made it to Julia Creek late that morning. After a rest of an hour and drink for me and the horses at that creek, I asked for directions to Lindfield, which wasn't really necessary as the horses were keen to get going. They knew where home was. We arrived at the station at about 9.30 that evening. I let the horses go in the horse paddock after giving Ched a good brush down, dragging my aching body to my quarters. Did anyone care if I got back safely?

It had to be a world record ride by my reasoning but it was a long, hard journey. Time and distance were not accurate, I could only estimate but the ride was done.

We were lucky, a brief window of a couple of weeks of fine, hot, humid weather, was building up to the Big Wet. Rain. You think you know about rain in the southern states. That's only drizzle. Here in Northern Queensland, its heavy, constant and goes on for weeks. It's not cold, just wet, boggy, damp and wet. You just have to stay put, travelling even short distances is out. Injury, sickness, medical help, sorry you just better treat yourself. Ambulances can't move; planes can't land. Helicopters, what are they? All busy in Vietnam. Rain, not letting up for two weeks, my quarters had half an inch of water on the floor. What happens after rain? Mosquitoes, they're huge. They even carry hurricane lanterns to find you. Sandflies, where there is no sand. Frogs trying out their vocal cords, singing from high to low notes. Rivers and creeks swollen and flooded; open plains turned to oceans. Yes, the Big Wet.

On a sunny morning, Barry came over and asked me if I could swim.

"Yes," I said, "why?"

"I thought you may like to come for a picnic with us down on Alick Creek."

I should have been cautious as it was rare for a station manager to ask a lowly stockman to join the family for a picnic. Me, as always, willing to please and being obliging said, "Yes, I'll come." Not thinking there might be an alternative motive in the invitation.

The rain had stopped but the roads were still dicey to travel on. The ute was full of picnic gear, or so I thought, with Barry, Reg and me jammed into the front of the Holden. With Barry and Reg's wives following in their car, I thought two cars were sensible travelling on muddy station roads.

We came to a raging torrid of water; Alick Creek was in full flood with lots of debris floating past. A picnic spot. It soon became clear, when Barry said, "Peter, his wife and three young children are stuck on the other side and have run out of rations."

I then noticed big Peter standing beside a huge gum tree on the other side of the raging torrent.

"We want you to swim to the other side with a rope so we can rig up a flying fox to send the food over to him."

Me, swim? What, no picnic? Jack's been conned again. Me swim that wild flooded creek? Not on your Nellie. I have only swum at the council baths in Kew and splashed around in the shallows at St Kilda beach.

"Ahh, Barry, I said I could swim a bit, but not in that." I pointed to the foaming, muddy, surging water with all the flood refuse going past.

"Well Jack, Reg and I can't swim, neither can Colin and Len."

Oh, how convenient, I thought.

"So, it's up to you to help Peter's family survive with the rations we have brought," said Barry, "We are depending on you to take a rope across. Look Jack, I'll give you $100 if you can do it."

One hundred quid! A fortune. I had already sent my month's wages to Mrs Thompson and the boys who loaned me the money to get here, so 100 bucks would be a good saving start for Joan and me. We only managed to send a couple of letters to each other due to the droving trip and the wet.

"All right, I'll give it a go." My thoughts, of course, were for poor Peter's starving marooned family. Why, what else did you think?

I walked up stream for about 100 metres in my shorts with a one-inch rope tied around my waist with a slip knot. I plunged into the washing machine on agitate. The current just grabbed me and pummelled me down the roaring, boiling water. The bloody rope was also caught in the force and pulling me down. I must untie this rope, Wack! A small branch got me on the shoulder. The rope, the so-called slip knot, was not slipping. I was drowning. A mouthful of muddy water, breath gone, strength gone, not long now. Goodbye Joan.

The slip knot slipped; the rope was gone. I landed on the other side of the flooded creek. I laid in the mud; the creek bank wasn't there. I caught my breath; I thought I had lost it. My lungs hurt, so did my shoulder, then I managed to find myself again. I hobbled up to Peter as the ground was not friendly to my soft, bare feet.

"I thought you were a goner, I was yelling for them to pull you back, but I don't think they heard me. When they saw you disappear, they then decided to pull the rope in but, of course, you were not on it. Jack thanks for trying, but I really thought you were a goner," exclaimed a very worried man. "You will have to swim back to the other side and find out what Barry can do. We are really out of food. The Wet caught us short."

Swim back? Oh my God, could I? I suppose I must. I walked back up the creek, 200 metres or so and plunged in. I decided not to swim to the other side directly but manoeuvre myself in the current with my eyes set on a dead tree about 100 metres from where Barry and Reg were standing. I made it.

Walking up to Barry, I said, "You can stick your 100 bucks. I'm finished. Find some other way to get the rope across. I'm buggered; I've done my best."

"There is a thermos of tea and some sandwiches in the back of the ute, please help yourself. Reg and I will see if we can get something across to Peter and thanks for trying." Barry turned to his brother suggesting, "If we tie a rock to some fishing line and try and swing that across."

"Nuh, it's too wide. What about getting a tyre tube and Jack could ride that?"

Hearing that, I yelled, "Fat chance."

Then Barry suggested a bow and arrow.

"We could shoot a line across, but we haven't got one."

They talked amongst themselves while I enjoyed the corn beef and pickled sandwich with the mug of tea. After a good half hour, they both enquired if I had enjoyed the rest and sandwich. And suggested I looked much better after the rest. Barry asked, more like begging, "Jack, you did make it across and back. We have no alternative but to employ you to try again."

"Well, you can forget about tying a bloody rope around me. Maybe if we tie a fishing line around a stick and carry that across and if I get caught, I can just let it go."

They both jumped at the idea.

"Good on ya Jack, then you will do it?"

I glanced across the swollen creek, in name only, now a fully flooded river. Not only did I see Peter, but standing by his side, was his wife Barb and three sweet little girls holding on to their mummy and daddy's hands. Did I have a choice? No, the food had to be sent across.

I walked up stream again, a few hundred yards, holding the stick with the line attached high above my head. Reg followed me, holding the line up as well, so we didn't get it snagged on the ground. I went in again, aiming for the other side. Just a few yards in, something violently snatched the line out of my hand. I guess, a branch or something floating down got caught in it. I made it to the other side again, alive but no line.

Barb mentioned how brave I was and one little girl asked if she was having any supper. Buggar. Again, the swim, the line, the negating the debris and a floating beast. There is no need for me to go on about exhaustion, near death experiences and my bravery. But on my fifth swim I made it.

They tied their end of the line on to the rope while Peter pulled it in and tied it about 12 feet above on the large tree. Barry did the same but much higher at his end, so gravity would work. A snatch block pully was attached to the rope and a large box to it. At the bottom of the box was attached another rope which Barry held to slow the travelling box and to pull it back to his side. In other words, a flying fox.

All the goods were successfully transferred across. Two of the little girls wanted to go for a ride in the flying fox but mother said a stern "No." I, having had a good rest, was to swim back across the other side, my sixth crossing. It was not practical for me to go via flying fox. The last crossing was as dangerous as the first, because the current or the flow was 10 times stronger or was I 10 times weaker? Who knows?

The operation was successful. Peter and his family could enjoy meals again. The rope was replaced with a permanent steel cable and Jack, did he get a bravery award from the governor or mentioned in dispatches? No. The $100? Barry said I told him to stick it, so he did, in his pocket. But I was happy. I had helped a hungry family and knew when the odds were down, I could succeed.

We were lucky to get supplies across to Peter as the next day the rain came for the next 10 days. The roads were completely impassable. Colin, who had shifted, with his wife, down to Losborn Station to be a boundary rider, was now out of supplies. What was there to be done? The management thought, *Well, we will get Jack to take Colin some supplies.*

"Jack, we have a good job for you tomorrow, but you will have to have an early start."

"And what death-defying job is that going to be?"

"No Jack, nothing like the other week. It's just Colin and his wife are short of rations and you would be just the man to take some down to them."

"How am I going to do that? The roads are impassable. There is just no way, Losborn is at least 27 kilometres away."

Early the following day, here I was on Lucy, leading two big half draft horses, Ben and Dan, with pack saddles on them full of the needs for Colin and partner. Six-thirty on a light showery morning the expedition started. Managing Lucy and two horses with large pack saddles, just getting through gates was an ordeal. The walking of horses through a thick, wet, muddy track, was hard enough as well. You might imagine, the horses' feet, covered with black soil, were as big as stump caps. I was about a few kilometres, looking back at the track, I noticed in the distance the windmill and Barry on the top of the tower with binoculars, checking on my progress. I don't know whether he could see me, but I gave him the finger salute anyway.

It was a long hard slog, arriving at about 6.45 that evening. Colin and his wife, Kate, were over the moon to see me. They had not eaten for two days. They had tried to get to town a few times to get stores but were unsuccessful. It must be remembered that pay day is once a month by cheque and for a young, married couple it's very difficult for them to hold a store of food for emergency times. They felt uncomfortable asking for help as they thought they might have a chance for town the next day. And adding to the problem was the phone, a party line which often didn't work when wet.

After taking the supplies in for Kate to unpack, Colin helped me to unsaddle the horses, gave them a good rub down and feed. Then we rolled a cigarette, had a yarn. He told me how he survived the droving trip and how Kate was by herself at that time.

"No, she was fine," said Colin, "didn't you know she stayed with her mum in town while we were away? There is no way I'd leave her by herself, she would be spooked." (I will tell you about that later when I had an experience down there when Colin and Kate were away).

It was a very late dinner that night. Kate did an excellent job cooking a meal. She was very excited with all the goodies I brought. There was kerosene for the large permeant hanging lamp and blocks of carbine for the smaller carbine lamps. Poor things had been living in the dark for a few days as well as having no food. It was a good night for the three of us just having relaxing company, which we seldom had.

I stayed the next day to give the horses a rest and to help Colin fix a few things to help them settle in, as they had only started at Lindfield a few days before me. With the droving trip starting straight away, that hadn't given them much time to settle into their new positions.

Back at the main homestead, everything was drying out. Going to bed this night with all the open downs, the country was bare of grass or anything, except for the mimosa bushes growing along the bore drain. Waking up the next morning, would you believe, a miracle? All was green as far as the eye could see. Yes, green grass, herbage, wildflowers, it was unbelievable.

It is difficult to contemplate such growth could happen so quickly, how the country responds to life giving rain. Of course, other things responded, such as flies and rats. Yes, rats. A plague of hundreds and thousands of rats. They ate suitcases, saddles, anything and everything their gnawing horrible teeth could get into. Traps of all kinds, new ideas on drowning them, poisoning, shooting with rat shot, jumping on them, all the methods worked, but there were too many of them to make a difference.

After the rats came the cats. No, not lovely little pussies but big strong felines. Sorry, I tried to run over one, but it turned around and attacked the car. Fair dinkum! Yes, we survived.

We went back and mustered the 6,000 weaners and maiden ewes we drove earlier that month and did a count. Reg and Mr Molloy confirmed a count of 5,620 head. The ten we lost in the break and the others we pulled out, probably didn't survive. We sold them to Mr Molloy, who now had plenty of feed, for an undisclosed amount.

Interestingly, we met a man, the day before the rain, in a ute heading towards Julia Creek, who told us he was driving 3,500 ewes and was tired and out of money. A grazier offered him half a cent a sheep, so he sold them to him. The grazier would have made a lot of money now there had been rain. I guess sometimes a gamble pays off.

Barry's ewes were brought back to Lindfield eight weeks after we had good rain and plenty of feed. He had contracted a team to drive them back.

C.3

Spiders, Snakes, Bites, Accidents

Small, thin, likeable Colin. He was one of those chaps that was accident prone. If anyone had a mishap, it was he. Digging a deep hole for a strainer post, he couldn't clean it out properly. He laid down to get the rest of the dirt out of the hole when he was bitten by a strange spider on the hand. He had the presence of mind to capture it in a cloth. Starting to feel quite faint, he managed to drive home, where he collapsed in the car. Kate ran out and, without thinking, pushed Colin to the other side of the car and hightailed it to the hospital some 60 kilometres away, where they took the semi-conscience man out of the car. Later that day, the Flying Doctor came and took him and the spider, which was now in a jar, straight to a Brisbane hospital. Colin was a very sick man and it was believed he could die.

Three weeks later he was back home and I borrowed the station ute with some supplies for a not very well looking Colin and a very worried Kate. Colin said it was identified as an American black widow spider. I said, "Aren't they just our normal redback spiders that live in cracks and underneath dunny seats, but not that dangerous?"

"Well come and have a look at this one," Colin said.

He had it on the mantle-piece in a jar, of course. He handed it down to me. I saw a dangerous-looking black spider, much bigger than any redback I had seen and it did not have a red stripe or mark on it anywhere. I put an HB pencil in. The thing grabbed it with its fangs and I could feel the strength of it as I pulled the pencil out. I noticed on the brown and white end of the pencil, the spider's fangs had put two grooves in it, down to the bare wood. Extraordinary, seeing the spider presumably had been in the jar for a month and still had that strength.

Another item on Colin's mantle, was a mounted horseshoe.

"What is that about?" I said, pointing to it.

"Oh, that was on the hoof of a horse that kicked me in the groin and I lost one of my testicles."

"Gee, I did not know you copped that, can you still have kids?'

"The doc said I could. It happened six months ago," he said, "I'm feeling ok now but perhaps a bit lopsided." Colin grinned.

I also noted another jar next to the others. It was large with a very big snake coiled in some preserving liquid. I did not need to ask him about the snake, because I was there when that event happened.

Colin had been walking along the bore drain, probably dreaming, saw the snake and jumped in the air in fright, then landed on it, as only Colin would. The snake struck and caught his fangs in Colin's thick jeans. He bent down and grabbed the serpent by the back of the neck and pulled it off his jeans, leaving a poison's trace on them.

Now, the problem for poor Colin was, he held the snake, later identified as an inland taipan, by the neck as the rest curled tightly around his arm. He didn't know what to do next. How could he get rid of a very angry snake?

So, what did our hero do? Well, I'll tell you. He walked six kms to the homestead. How he held on to the thing all that time, beats me. He was yelling, "Help! Help!"

We heard the cries as we were eating lunch. We rushed out to see the cause. Barry must have heard the cries as well; he tumbled out the door too. And here was poor Colin, covered in sweat and fear, saying, "What do I do with this?"

As he held his arm out, showing us his problem, Barry said, in the calmest of voices, "Colin, just bend down, put the snake's head on the ground and crush it with your boot."

Which he did, saying, "I never thought of doing that."

Poor bloke. We offered him lunch and a mug of tea to get him relaxed over his ordeal. It was suggested that he should wash the poison off his jeans. We all checked out his bare leg to see if any bite marks were visible. He was lucky, a bite from that snake, without emergency intervention, would have been fatal. I wonder what else will end up on his mantlepiece with the bottled snake, the jarred spider and the horseshoe, I forgot, there was an appendix in another jar, adding to the collection.

We used to jump over white coloured snakes, thinking they were harmless grass snakes. We soon learnt different when one of the sheep dogs was attacking one of them and was bitten on the tongue. Within a fraction of a second, the dog flew in the air and was dead when it hit the ground. What disturbs me to this day, when something dies, they look at peace. This dog didn't. It had pain and agony etched on his face after we left him. They were not grass snakes; they were brown snakes camouflaged by the dry grass.

I must tell you what happened about a new man on the job. Instead of a swag, he had a sleeping bag. Now a swag is very easy to get out of, it's like a bed, pull the covering to one side and out you go. In an emergency like a cattle rush, fire or flood, they are easy to get out of, but a sleeping bag can take some time to be free. As was in this case.

It was my turn to cook breakfast. I got up just as daylight

was breaking, to gather some kindling to light the fire, when I noticed the new man, Reg, in his sleeping bag, signalling me. Using one arm, he was pointing to his sleeping bag and kept doing it. I thought he was a restless sleeper or something, so I got busy getting the fire going and putting the billy on. I glanced over and he was still pointing to his sleeping bag. It was early and being a bit disturbed from my job, I eventually walked over to him and said, "What's wrong with you?"

He pointed again to the centre of his bag and I noticed a large lump. I said, 'What's that, a snake?" He slowly moved his head up and down in the gesture of a yes. "So, it's a snake in your sleeping bag, is it?" Another nod.

I woke the other fellas up and said, "Guess what, Reg has a snake in his sleeping bag. As they scrambled out of their swags, the billy was boiling, so I chucked a couple of handfuls of tea in, knowing they would want a cuppa before deciding how to help poor Reg out of his predicament.

As we squatted down by the fire with our mugs of hot tea, one of the chaps suggested we get the flat of a shovel and bash the Christ out of the snake. That suggestion was discarded. Another was, "Why don't we carefully cut the bottom of the bag and smoke the bastard out?"

We thought that was ok, then someone said, "But that would get Reg coughing and cause trouble with the snake."

At last, a sensible suggestion was forwarded, "Snakes don't like a lot of heat, so why don't we carefully put all our swags and anything else we got and gently put them all on Reg's swag. The weight and heat of it all would have to draw the snake out."

Good idea, then we proceeded to do just that. After I put my gear on top of Reg's sleeping bag, I reboiled the billy then proceeded to put the chops on, for our breakfast. I walked over to the chaps who were squatting beside Reg, waiting to see if there was any movement in the bag.

The sun was getting up in the sky and I could see the trickle of sweat running down Reg's face.

"It won't be long now," I said to no one in particular, "I've made a fresh brew of tea and the chops should be about ready, I'll make some toast later on."

Quick, there was movement. We grabbed our chops and mugs and squatted beside Reg to see the great event. The snake slowly uncoiled itself and made its way to the bottom of the bag, then finding no way out it continued its journey to the small bit of light beside Reg's neck. The head came out, the tongue flicking in and out, sensing the air. It didn't like the atmosphere as it could sense us sitting so close. It decided to go back where it was safe.

We all moved back several metres; we were just too close before. We discussed what type of snake it was. Definitely not a python, had to be a brown, was the conclusion.

"Heya Jack, where is the toast?"

"Sorry fellas, I will get on to it right away."

"Forget it, the snake is on its way out now."

We held our breaths. We didn't move as the snake slowly slid along Reg's neck and out of the sleeping bag. Berty grabbed the shovel and dispatched the five- and half-foot brown snake.

I checked on Reg. He was in a semi-conscious state. We all took our swags off the sleeping bag and pulled Reg out, which wasn't easy. I gave him some slight slaps on the cheek to bring him around and yelled, "Bring us some water and a mug of tea for Reg."

After giving him the water, he sat up, sipping his tea and I asked him, "How long had the snake been there?'

He said, "Not long after we went to bed, guess half to an hour."

"Gee, you mean it was with you all night?"

"Yes Jack. Look mate, I don't feel well, I am feeling fuzzy and a bit out of it."

"Did the bastard bite you?"

"I don't think so." Then he just fell back, spilling his tea.

"Fellas get the ute, I'm taking him to the hospital, now. Reg is out of it."

We never saw Reg again. We know he wasn't bitten and he left the hospital a few days later. I wonder if his first purchase was a swag. Or did he decide to go to New Zealand where they don't have snakes, only Kiwis?

Accidents: no, better described as misadventures, like turning my back in the cattle yard to get out. A wild micky bull is one that has not been mustered, branded or castrated yet. This particular one charged and his sharp horn caught me on the bum, ripping my britches. It was a close call. I was pulled out of the yard by Reg and he said he saved my life. But they all wanted to check the rip in my jeans, more like me bum. I was lucky, the loose jeans stopped the horn from doing any real damage, but I had a very long red mark that was causing me some discomfort, probably muscle damage.

A big horse, 16 odd hands, was given to me to ride. His name was, No Name, and this horse could buck. After first saddling up, I would ride him round and round the horse yard and he wouldn't do anything. I tried to make him buck but he would not have a bar of it. No, in his own good time. Like a hard morning's mustering, just finished lunch, mounted him; he would get stuck into it and throw me like a fly. If it was after lunch or smoko, it would be near the homestead after a big day.

When he decided to put on a turn, I could never stay on him. Once he had thrown me, which he always did, I would remount and he would be happy and not do anything after. To give you an idea of how strong he was, he threw me this day, the girth broke and the saddle came with me. I was still in the saddle, spurring like mad but on the ground. The other blokes laughing at my predicament, said, "Look at Jack, he can ride a mean horse while on the ground."

If ever there was a rodeo within a couple of hundred kms, I would go and nominate for the bull ride and saddle bronc. I have never tried the bareback ride. This particular rodeo was at Kynuna. The bull I drew was a poly black mean beast. I screwed down on him, the rope tied tight round my right wrist, my left hand in the air.

I shouted, "Open the gate," and then it was on, not too bad, a few good bucks a couple of twists and turns, riding him to his rhythm, a crack of the stock whip, I had made time. Yea, and then all went black.

The next thing, while dazed, there were two men beside me arguing, "You can't leave him here, drag him back behind the chutes and let him recover or die there. It's no good for the show to have someone injured on the ground and it's slowing up the event."

"No, we can't move him till he regains consciousness."

"It's okay fellas," I said, struggling up on to my feet, dazed.

They helped be back to the chutes, where I recovered with a huge bump and a bit of blood on my forehead, but alive. I must have leant too far forward to get off the bucking beast and the poll at the top of his head must have collided with mine.

Later on that day, I had ridden a great horse that helped me put on a good show. I was pleased with my success, as I rode both my animals in time. Besides the bump on my head, it to me, was a great day.

I found out later, there was a big fight with the locals that night at the Blue Healer Pub after I had gone home. It seemed that the locals thought I should have gotten a high place in both my rides but seeing I was a local, the A.R.R.A. (Australian Rough Riders Association) were the professional riders with their own judges. They did not like locals outdoing them and their prize money, even though they took my membership fee and nomination fee. I did not know anything about it till I went to nominate at a Richmond Rodeo and was told I was disqualified from riding.

"Why?" I asked.

"Because you cause fights and trouble for the association."

I answered truthfully that I was unaware of any fights or trouble caused with the A.R.R.A. Later I got the real story, surprisingly, from Barry.

C.4

Station Life, Joan, Leaving

We got a new cook, Dawn. She was a much better cook than Susan but let's leave it at that. She had family in Richmond and they all worked on different stations doing the work that was required of them. Dawn was a big girl and could handle herself but she had a sweet nature and being the cook, I made it my business to get on well with her. She asked me what my favorited pudding was and I told her - chocolate blancmange with raisins. Well, that was a bit of a mistake as we had it for sweets for weeks and the fellas whinged about it and told me never ask for a certain favourite dish.

One day, as a joke, I said to Dawn, who also made our lunches, "Look, there is a bit of pudding left over. I might as well have it for lunch."

Nothing was said the next day while out mustering we had a break for lunch. I noticed in my lunch of slightly toasted sandwiches, which were wrapped in newspaper and bounced around in our saddle bags in 40 degrees of hot humid weather, another package. In it was a little plastic sealed dish with a little plastic spoon. The contents were my chocolate blancmange with some tin peaches in it. I said to the fellas, "I think I'll have some pudding now," and with all my humanity, I slurped the lot in front of them.

It was a great treat. I should have eaten it in secret but that's not in my nature. Poor Dawn. She got into trouble over it.

"And no more lunch time pudding for the men," instructed the boss.

There was a Bachelor and Spinsters ball advertised and Dawn wanted to go. She asked me to partner her and said that Barry would lend us the Zephyr car to go to the ball. I agreed but I was short of a suit. That was fixed up.

"You can wear my brother's. He is your size," said Dawn.

And so it was, off to the ball. A big problem, the band was paid to play till midnight. The hall was near the pub but the problem was, there were hardly any girls. About one girl to every 20 blokes. Well, the girls vanished quickly. What to do? Go over to the pub, practically buy all the grog, bring it over to the hall and drink to midnight, while the band played.

Dawn met her friend, a drover from Dalgonally Station, Tiddly Triffid, who I had casually met beforehand.

"Stuff this," he said, "Come on Dawn and you, Jack, let's get out of here."

And so we did, after Tiddly grabbed a few bottles of whisky. We drove out to the town common and just yarned in the car front bench seat, passing the whisky bottles around. Dawn was just one of us men, joining in, telling bush yarns, a few drunken songs we knew, lied about everything and we all had a good, inebriated time.

Tiddly hopped out of the car, sometime late in the evening and said, "You kids better get home. I'll just take a walk from here."

We drove home. No, we woke up in the middle of a paddock. We had fallen asleep and had run off the road. Thank God it was open downs and no objects to hit. But where were we?

"Dawn, could you hop out and see if you can see our tyre tracks?"

"Yea, I got it," she yelled. "Okay, I'll turn the car around and we should be able to follow them back to the road," and so we did.

Trouble was, Dawn had to have breakfast and lunches cut by 6am and me with Paul, a new station hand, had to be ready to go mustering by 6.45am. Does that seem a problem? Sure was, as Dawn and I got back to the station at 5.10 am. Panic for both of us. Our breakfast was yuk, so were our lunches. Poor Dawn, as she had to not only cook for the four of us men but for the boss and his wife, as well.

Mustering, riding on a jerky horse, with my brain swimming around in my skull, the sun burning my eyeballs, I kept them shut most of the time, hoping the horse knew what do. I probably missed sheep. Oh, my head ached so much. I wished the horse could float. I came to the conclusion I was very sick. My diagnosis was probably a hangover from the previous couple of hours.

We had more staff. Paul, the station hand, was a happy chap, rather plump, but a hard worker considering his body shape. Alan Readon, a small wiry man with a menacing type of face, small eyes, tight mouth, only talked when he had to. Slept in the room next to mine and was employed as the horse breaker. And then, you know Bob, the cowboy, that'd been here for ages.

Now this horse breaker, Alan, must have had childhood problems that manifested into adulthood. He would sleep soundly, but if you had to wake him up, which was quite often, he would spring out of bed and start throwing lethal punches. So, waking him up was a process. A person with straw broom in hand, would stand behind the doorway, leaning forward, then start poking him with the broom. When woken, he would fly out of bed throwing those punches. The person waking him up was normally me and I would quickly evacuate the quarters before an injury was sustained.

Because I complained about no toilet, I was given the job of digging one. With crowbar, pick and shovel, I started the job. When black soil is cooked in the burning sun it has to be chipped out as if its gravel. Not an easy job but after a good week, I managed to dig a hole, eight feet deep and six by four wide, as there was a back-to-back toilet already made to put over the hole, which I did. During the digging, I was thinking, I had the right to launch the first poo and christen the hole. Also, I was going to time it to see how long the bomb would take before it hit the bottom. I finished setting it up, went to get the toilet paper from my room, hurried back as the bomb was primed and, to my utter horror, Bob walked out of my new toilet and said it was urgent; he didn't have time to run to the trees. I was angry. How dare he have the first poop in my toilet. I could have throttled his scrawny neck.

I suppose you want to hear about my love life with Joan? I had saved a lot of money. Barry paid all my monthly wages into my bank account, so I didn't spend any of it. When my riding trousers wore out, I made them into shorts; when the shorts wore out, I made small leggings to keep seed from sticking to my socks; when my shirts wore out, I made handkerchiefs. I used old razor blades to shave and used other people's soap left in the shower.

I even asked Barry for extra work on weekends for cash. I chopped and poisoned Mimosa bushes along the bore drains. A difficult job considering the large thorns covering the branches. Then the hard filthy job, was shearing three hundred odd cancerous sheep. These would have huge stinking cancers on their faces and ears. The job was to shear them, then slit their throats and skin them. The money was good. I was mean; I was desperate to have a bank together. No more being poor.

Now, to my darling Joan. I wrote to her every week. She wrote to me most weeks. We had to rely on the once-a-week mail and the wet. She even sent me a coconut from South Moll Island and had a great trip to Sydney. Was she looking at wedding dresses? All was good. The letters of undying love spoke of not being able to wait to see me again. A week after my 21st birthday, I got rather a short letter from Joan saying:

Dear Jack, I have fallen in love with Terry and we are engaged. Sorry to have to write this, but hope you are not too angry with me. Love Joan.

Not too angry, was an understatement. My loyalty to her, my saving for a beautiful life together. I always pictured us being together again. The bitch! While I was working in this stinking God-forsaken country, she eventually was playing up, having holidays, and "stuff you, Jack."

No, I wasn't 'too' angry, just terribly let down, with a feeling of a great loss. It took some time to recover from that short note, but I did. Boosting myself up by saying what a fabulous life she would miss out on. Some people must have their cake without the icing on top and in between. Of course, I was the icing. I destroyed her coconut by smashing it with a hammer and eating the contents and burning all her letters and photo. And as far as I was concerned, there never was a Joan.

So, in my grief, I found a pet, a little budgerigar with a broken wing. I splinted it and cared for it, hoping it would fly again. I took loving care of him. I even named him, Flinders, but he died and now he is just cinders. I would love to have owned a dog but it wasn't practical under the conditions I was in. My work horses were my companions. Until Dawn heard of my bad news and decided that I might like a human companion; maybe her.

In the middle of the year in 1963, there was a huge celebration at the Combo Water Hole, near Kynuna. That great

Australian anthem, Waltzing Matilda by Banjo Patterson, who visited the waterhole, was probably based on a real incident that happened there in the 1890s. People came from miles around, in light planes, utes, trucks, posh cars, horses and buggies.

And yes, a Cobb and Co stagecoach arrived, which was celebrating 50, or was it 75, years when the coach ran. It had travelled from the gulf on its way to Melbourne. It was a huge turnout. My boss's father, Mr Sailen, drove the stagecoach in to the celebration as he had driven the coaches in his early years, with two ladies as passengers in period costume playing Waltzing Matilda on mouth organs.

The large crowd gathered and cheered as the coach, pulled by four horses, rolled in. Mr Sailen, a bit carried away by the occasion, tied the reins on to the break handle and was standing and waving to the crowd. His high-heeled riding boot caught on a rail of the coach and he went headfirst into the crowd. He was caught with no injuries, but it all added to the merriment of the occasion.

And what an occasion it was. A lot of volunteers worked tirelessly days before hand, to make it a huge success. On rolling spits, they cooked a beast: sheep, pork, goanna and all sorts of eats and fun. But the real surprise was, just on sunset, there was a call for all to come down to the waterhole.

We were all encouraged to sing Waltzing Matilda. As the throng sang, a swagman was sitting beside the water hole, boiling his billy, yes, under a coolabah tree. Then, out of nowhere, a sheep came down to drink. The swagman then stuffed the poor sheep into his tucker bag. A smart looking squatter came by on a prancing thoroughbred horse and with him was a trooper, number 123. The swagman jumped into the Combo waterhole. And from the coolabah tree, a ghost appeared. It was so well done in time with us all singing in tune. Wonderful memories I will never forget.

A note. With the stagecoach travelling to the Combo, there just had to be an armed robbery. The culprits were caught a couple of weeks later and so a mock trial was held with a real magistrate, who asked the witness how she identified the culprit. She replied, "I know the rascal well, I used to smack his bottom often when he was a child."

The magistrate then said, "Could you recognise his bottom for the court?"

She replied, "Yes, your Honour."

Then the robber had to show his bare bum to the court room. Fun times.

For a while, I took over Colin's job as a boundary rider at Losborn Station. It was very lonely being by oneself for a few months. I always admire people who do great adventures, not the adventures themselves, but dealing with one's loneliness. Not having seen a soul for three weeks, I was away with the fairies repairing a fence, miles from anywhere, when I heard a voice say, "G'day."

I had to be dreaming but turned around anyway. I got the shock of my life, when I saw a real man standing there. My heart was pounding as I said rather sharply, "Where in the hell did you come from?"

"Sorry to give you a start. I'm Fredrick, the council dogger."

"Where did you spring from?" I asked this Fredrick, who was bare-footed, shaggy beard, dirty shirt and shorts, dog traps hanging from a strap and carrying a rifle.

"I got a camp 'bout two mile back, seen any tracks around?"

"No, sorry."

Then he just moved on, as I was still getting over the whole encounter.

At Losborn, there was an old house and a cottage for a married couple. Now the house just had to be haunted, no one had lived in it for years. It must have once been a rather grand homestead, but now it was decaying. Me, being very brave, had a look around at midday, as I had not heard of ghosts being active at that time. It was creepy; I had an eerie feeling; I wanted to run but I held my nerve with my 12-gauge shotgun at the ready.

There were bits of furniture laying around, a couple of once grand leather armchairs in the lounge but the leather was rotten and the stuffing was half out on the floor. I felt something light moving on the back of my neck. I swung around, gun ready to blast something. The tangle of large spider webs, caught around my neck, made the gun useless. The place was a mist of spider webs, in every room. It took me ages to get them off my shoulders and body.

There were eyes everywhere, looking at me from the four quarters of the large dining room. The eyes where hidden in old, large, wooden frames belonging to Boer War and First World War soldiers. Were they killed in those conflicts, or did they survive to an old age? I didn't care, I was out of there before skeletal hands grabbed me and took me to their lair.

It was unnerving. I was sitting on the steps of the cottage, having a much-needed smoke, trying to settle my nerves down. But the nerves were not settling down, as the westerly wind blowing through the group of Athel pine trees made a wooooo, wooooo, WOOOOOO sound. Scary, but not as scary as the outside dunny. There was something in there. The door kept moving; it weren't no wind. It was something or someone. (Remember I had been completely alone without a sight or word to anyone. One feels things. The brain is not working in an educated world; it's gone primitive rather quickly). What spirit was in the toilet? I did a wide circuit of the little building, creeping, till I was at the back of it, with shotgun ready. I moved quickly and softly and then, reaching with my right arm, I slammed the door open. A white blur flew out of the corrugated iron toilet. A sheep had been caught behind the door.

I was to be there for another two weeks. *Could I last? Would I be normal when I got back to Lindfield or would the green-overalled people take me away to an asylum?* No, I was still there!

Time went by quickly with more adventures, big cattle drives, big shearing jobs, having lots of experiences and learning like I had never learnt before. I had a thirst for knowledge, which I did not have when at school. I studied about livestock husbandry; I studied the best ways of building yards, about waters, bores, windmills and dams. Hungerford's veterinary volume was a constant friend. I drove my mother mad as she was supplying the books I needed. I asked anyone and everyone about the industry I was in. Most were only too happy to expound their knowledge, unfortunately some ignored me, saying that's what they went to university for. Surprisingly, they might have been well studied but weren't that very intelligent or practical to my way of thinking. Someone said, "There is nothing wrong with being ignorant, its staying ignorant, that's the problem."

I will never drink whisky again as long as I lived. Why? It happened this way. The three of us, Tiddly, Jimmy, and me, had just finished a long droving trip. We were thirsty, dirty and unkempt. We visited Gannon's Hotel and ordered three beers. The publican placed three schooners down and said, "These are the last drinks you get. You all smell really bad, I'll lose customers. Go upstairs, have a shower and clean yourselves up." Which we did.

We ended up having a big drinking session. Mr Gannon slammed three bottles of Johnney Walker whiskey down, saying, "I'm sick and tired of hearing how much you fellas think you can drink. Well, drink these. If you are still standing at closing time, it's my shout. If you can't, you pay double."

Putting a challenge like that to three young fellas, was a bit too much. We just then had to bet who would finish their bottle first.

I don't remember much, but I think Jimmy and I must have been taken to the hospital to be pumped out. Later the next day, after being discharged, we found Tiddly in the gutter. How long he had been there, I don't know, but he couldn't have been there a whole night and day. Just the smell of whisky now makes me feel sick.

Mystery: Barry came in at breakfast and said, "I have been on the phone with the police and there is a man missing. Jack, take Paul and Allan with you, after saddling your horses and ride to the boundary on the Julia Creek/Neila boundary. Do a thorough search of the area. You better take your lunches with you. I have not many details, but it is an old man with a coloured check shirt missing. He reportedly got out of the car to check on something; the wife, still in the car, was found early this morning still waiting for him. She is now at Julia Creek. We rode up and down that paddock within sight of each other all day and part of the next, but nothing was found. I mean, really, an open paddock with no trees or scrub, no dam or creek to fall in? If there was a person or body to be found, we would have found it."

The story we found out later was, the elderly couple were seen leaving Neila that afternoon. As they were driving along the road, the woman said to her husband, "Stop the car, I can hear someone yelling for help."

They stopped the car and the woman said to her husband, "You better look for that person in trouble."

He did and was never seen again.

Our questions were: How could anyone hear a call for help in a car travelling along a dirt pothole road with the windows up? What happened to the man? Martians perhaps. Did the woman knock her husband off and dump him somewhere else? Or was it just a story the woman told to the police?

A couple of interesting stories Reg told me. True? Maybe.

It was during the drought before I was there. The community pestered the local minister to hold a special service to pray for rain. The minister was not keen on the idea at all, as his golf day was the Wednesday the community chose for the service. The community was so insistent, as they were desperate for rain and the church was their last hope. And so, it was.

They came for miles around that day to the prayer meeting. The minister was late as they waited outside the church talking and getting a bit apprehensive about him not arriving but he did, with golf clubs sticking outside of the passenger side window of his car. Without getting out of the car, he loudly spoke to his parishioners, "None of you have faith in the Lord to pray for rain, as none of you have brought an umbrella," so off he went to play his game of golf. Reg said he didn't last long as the minister.

Another story I was not aware of, during the wet, no matter what, a burial had to be performed as soon as a person died, as there were no freezers or places to keep a corpse. Now, the grave had been dug but, unfortunately, the small gathering to say goodbye was surprised to see the grave full of water and the coffin would not sink. Someone whispered, "You can't keep a good man down."

The minister opened the trunk of his car and pulled out a brace and bit, then with the help of the funeral director, turned the coffin on its side and drilled holes into the bottom of it. Everyone had their eyes glued to the bit as it was withdrawn, hoping nothing was attached to it. But the coffin sank and everyone was happy as you could be at a funeral, as the problem had been solved.

To give you an idea of how isolated we were, not having newspapers, radios full of static and news of the world were not part of our education. In 1963, Pope John XXIII died in June and President John F. Kennedy was assassinated in November of that year. I was not aware of these events for some time.

I was getting restless, so it was time to move on. Barry had bought his own place, Hampton Downes, which Colin and I decided to help him get established by crutching and shearing fly-blown sheep he had bought cheap. I don't know about buying, more like sheep left in the sale yard no one wanted. But some wool and a lamb was a good start to owning a good financial flock.

Barry with his new property, Reg moving down to New South Wales to manage a property there, it was time. I hadn't seen my family for over two years, so with money in the bank, I flew straight to Melbourne, which was a mistake.

C.5

Melbourne, Ardglen, Clevelane.

I arrived at 9.30pm by A.N.A on Saturday night, a very long flight. A changeover in Townsville and a short stop in Sydney to pick up more passengers. I kept to myself on the flights; I did not feel like talking to these strange people. They had come from some other planet, it seemed.

We landed at Essendon Aerodrome. As we were parked to let all the passengers off, I did not want to move. I could see my mother, grandmother and my sister with her new husband on the viewing platform. I thought, *I have seen them now, might as well stay here and fly back to Queensland.* But of course, I couldn't. Being last out of the plane, I slowly walked across the tarmac to the arrival hall and then what I dreaded: hugs and sloppy kisses.

"My, how you have grown. You're so tanned, you've filled out a lot, look at those muscles, how did you break your front tooth?" and so it went on as I was mobbed to the baggage claim by my loving family.

Alright, I would have been disappointed if I was not made a fuss of, but still it was a bit awkward. Gran had made a nice supper with an iced sponge cake, which I don't remember having had since my last visit. The questions they asked, they didn't believe the true answers. They wanted the ones they expected or they believed about the outback, so I lied to satisfy them and they were happy. By the way, a ringer does not work for the telephone exchange. He is a gun shearer or a stockman. A station hand is not a porter at a railway station; he is a general hand on a sheep or cattle station.

On stations back then, there was a male social stratum. For example, a house boy was usually an Aboriginal boy from a mission who helped doing the house chores. Then the cowboy, who did chores outside the house, such as: milk the cows, kill the sheep, look after the chooks and garden, supplies firewood etc. There was the station hand who was a handyman doing fencing, yard building, stock work, mechanical, etc. Then the ringer/stockman who handled stock work and husbandry. Top of this tree was the head stockman.

Now, the other side of the social tree was the jackeroo, who was the apprentice. Then, maybe after four years, he would graduate to overseer; a few more years to station manager. Take a few more years, if he was lucky, he might become a pastoral manager who looked after a multitude of properties for large companies.

Then there were the individuals who specialised in their specific jobs, such as, windmill expert, mechanic / machine operator, fencer, yard builder, cooks, gardeners and so on. Sorry girls, but it was rare for girls in the outback, but when there was, they could do any jobs the men did. I have to admit, sometimes better. I haven't mentioned the shearers and the workers in a shearing shed. But you had to ask the team for permission for a woman to enter the shed when it was working. Women were not allowed in the public bar of hotels, either.

Of course, there were some cheeky fellas who could not wait to be promoted so they promoted themselves. *I'll apply for the job, if I keep it well and good, if I stuff up, well there is always another place.* I think I might have been one of the cheeky fellas, always wanting to be the boss.

Things were not right in Melbourne. The house had shrunk, so had the sleepout, my original bedroom. On the street, I walked down the middle of the road thinking my elbows would scratch the house fences on each side. After living for such a long time in great open plains, where you could see a windmill shimmering 60 kilometres away or horse men galloping in the sky due to a heat haze, everything else seemed small.

My mother suggested I go to the city and buy some decent clothes as I really didn't have any. She suggested I go to Henry Bucks, the specialist men's store, established 1890. The tram ride, actually handling money and sitting with people was frightening. Not as bad as when I was in the posh shop. A well-mannered, well-dressed gentleman approached me by saying in a well-educated voice, "How may I help you, Sir?"

I stammered saying, "I need strides, shirts, sports coat, the works."

He signalled to other attendants who carried shirts, trousers, coats and other paraphernalia, showing me all their wares in a displayed manner.

"Sir, this is a beautiful garment made by the best English cloth. Sir, I'm sure these type of trousers would suit you," said another gentleman.

I was terrified; I panicked. I flew out of the store, caught a taxi home, went straight to my den like a pursued wild animal. It took me sometime to assimilate to city life. Once, I was nearly done for exposure. Up north when the need arose, you just downed your trousers and did it. I started to do it in Collins Street and just remembered in time, cutting it short so the Sports Girl shopfront didn't get a liquid tattoo. Another thing I had to learn, was to hold it until I came to the appropriate place.

I went to the pictures and saw the Dr Zhivago film. I was

horrified when it came to the scene of him having intercourse. There happened to be two teenage girls sitting either side of me, so I was shocked. It was not my scene at all. What had happened to morality in the cities? I desperately wanted to go back to Queensland.

I did a stupid thing. My father bought a farm and asked me to help him. I did, but why? I think there was some queer psychology that happens to males who lose their fathers through divorce. Even if those fathers had nothing or very little to do with their sons. There seems to be something that attracts the son to the father again. What it is and why it happens, and it does, remains a mystery. I worked on his farm, ploughing, sowing, running waterpipes and putting troughs in, as well as helping with the dairy. Why he bought the place in his 60s and thought he had money when he didn't, beats me. Three months, no pay, I paid for an obligation that I felt and ended up telling him to shove it, politely.

I bought a second-hand Holden F.C. ute, my first car. Said goodbye to my mum and gran, and with great excitement drove myself back home to my Queensland. Mrs Thompson of Thompson Boarding House in Goondiwindi greeted me with open arms. I asked if there was any room at the inn and there was. Great! Next morning, down to the agent's office where I was offered a few jobs. I had telegrammed Mrs Gillespie at the Dalgety's office before leaving Melbourne. She said, "My, you must have made a good impression up north, we have a few jobs offered for you. Some from Julia Creek."

Barry from Lindfield had already offered me a job at Hampton Downes. One was near Cloncurry, another Mallapunyah Springs, Northern Territory as a stockman/manager. But I had enough up north, so I settled for an overseer's job at Ardglen, near Cunnamulla. (Rising up the ranks, pretty fast, aren't I?)

As I was washing my car, getting all the dirt and travelling stains off it, Mrs Thompson's daughter, Bev, a very large woman, about mid-30s, was doing the washing in the laundry on an old Pope washing machine with the wringer on top. She popped her head out and said, "Jack, when you're finished washing your car, could you take me to the hospital?"

"If its urgent I can take you now."

"No, it's okay, Jack. When you are finished."

Soon as I finished, I took Bev to the Goondiwindi hospital. I stopped at the entrance, and she opened the door and walked in. I drove back to the boarding house to clean the inside of my car. Sometime later that afternoon, Bev was finishing the washing and I noticed beside her was a bassinet with a little baby in it.

"Whose baby is that?" I asked,

"Who do you think it is? It's mine. Why did you think you took me to the hospital for?"

As I walked away a bit stunned, I said congratulations and thinking that's tough, doing the washing, having a baby, then finishing the washing. They made them tough out in the sticks.

The Governor, Sir Henry Abel Smith was coming to town. There was great excitement, it was rare such a distinguish person visited. I have forgotten the specific details, but it happened sometime in 1964/65. The yardman at the local pub was told to pick up the distinguished guest arriving by air at the Goondiwindi air strip. The yardman was not the brightest of chaps, but did what he was told, driving the boss' polished car to pick up the governor. Now I am not quite sure if the yardman knew who he was picking up.

Someone arriving by aeroplane had to be important. The yardman stiffly opened the passenger door to let the governor in, slammed it shut and started to drive in a stately manner back to the pub. Then, to his shock, he saw two police motorbikes following him. He panicked. He didn't have a licence and he was already in serious trouble with the local police. He did not understand, the police following, had ridden out from Brisbane to escort the governor while in Goondiwindi. He thought they were after him. He took off at an extremely fast rate and looked to see if he had lost the police. No, they were just behind him. He flattened the accelerator, took a broadside into the hotel's backyard and disappeared. The honourable Governor, Sir Henry Able Smith, had to extract himself from the car and make his own way to the reception held in his honour.

Later that year, I had the pleasure of having a connection with the Governor's wife, Her Excellency, May Able Smith. It was at the Cunnamulla sheep show, an important event and the governor and his wife were in the ring presenting the prizes for the best stud sheep. Now, it just so happened, well before the presentation, I was passing the small animal show ring looking at the stud sheep, when someone asked me if I knew anything about sheep. I assured him I did, then he asked me if I would be kind enough to hold a sheep for the upcoming presentation with the governor and his wife. I said, "Sure, why not? I had nothing better to do."

I was showed how to hold the stud ewe properly, by having the nose of the sheep between my legs, holding with both hands the cheek of the sheep, which I did. The governor and his wife arrived. As they were about to present the ribbons, my sheep suddenly butted me in the wrong place. I let the sheep go in pain, then realised it was such an official occasion that I rushed past the distinguished guests, connected with her ladyship, said I was sorry, caught the sheep and dragged it back very unceremonially to our original position, pretending nothing had happened. I often wondered if this incident caused me to miss out on a state award in later years.

It was a Tuesday when I accepted the job for a start on the following Monday. It was a good day's drive to Ardglen Station.

But that still gave me some R and R at Mrs Thompsons and a few beers with the fellas.

Ardglen was between Bollen and Cunnamulla on a very red sandy road which took a bit of navigation due to the postholes covered in sand, not to mention the corrugations. I arrived at four in the afternoon on Sunday, 31 May 1964. An oldish man appeared around the corner of the old shabby homestead, four days growth, sucking an orange, in working clothes that looked if they had been worked in, but had not. My God, he was the manager!

"Find yerself a room in the shearer's quarters, get settled, have a look around, the bell will ring at seven for dinner." I guess he knew I was the new overseer, no handshake, no introduction of names. Well, Jack, you have done it again.

I met the other workers. Wally at 19, was a good worker, short on brains, had been there 12 months and was now leaving. Graham, 20, a sound bloke and good worker. And Ben, part Aboriginal and a troublemaker. I noticed three disturbing things: a young pet emu in the house yard, a fox terrier dog, called Snitcher and a cockatoo chained on a perch who, every now and then, would call "Snitcher, Snitcher" and the dog would come running to see who was calling it. Finally, cats seemed to own the house yard. Jack, it does not seem this place is your cup of tea.

I met the Missus. Mrs Simpson, a kindly, plump lady, at last, who could cook, as the meal was plentiful and well prepared. We four men ate in the kitchen while Mr and Mrs Simpson retired to the dining room. After dinner and the men had been dismissed, Mr Simpson came and sat opposite me and told me about the job.

It appeared I was a sub overseer. Never heard of that title before and mentioned that to him. He explained the job was a trial and if the trial was successful, he would add another four dollars a week to the $40 I was to be paid now. Then I would be employed as an overseer. Then he explained chores. *Chores? I thought I was past chores.*

I had to milk the cow and get the horses in when required. The other men would chop the wood, kill for meat.

"I will relay the day's jobs to you the night before, then you will organise the men and make sure the jobs are done satisfactory. That is your job. Now breakfast is at seven, smoko is at 10 and three, dinner is seven pm. Times will change as the type of work does."

Ardglen was an interesting property of 80,000 acres. It was once one of the biggest stations in the area, but in the 50s, the government cut up all the big, leased properties to 40,000 thousand-acre holdings and sold them off as freehold. It was later found, much too late, that in mulga country you could not sustain a profitable living on that kind of limited acreage.

The owner, Mr Griffiths, bought two blocks. One held the great artesian bore which flowed through the two properties, using bore drains, that he held. But the blocks weren't joined together, so there was another holding in between them, called Heywood Station.

Work continued and two new windmills were erected. Mr Griffiths was a partner in Southern Cross windmills and he sent one of their employees to show and help me put one up and then I was on my own, after a long lecture on how to look after the windmills and repair the old ones, of which there were many on the property.

Employees changed quite often. An older man, Harry, about 63 years old, was employed for odd jobs. He had a lovely, plump Scottish wife, Clair, who was quite a character. I once asked her what she thought of the new fashion women were wearing, the plunging neckline. She replied with her quaint accent, "From a man's point of view, it should be looked down upon!"

Eventually, with a lot of goings and comings, I ended up with a great team of workers. Robert, 22 years, a good lanky worker who was fun to work with. His father used to manage proprieties in the area, so he knew the country. Keith was about 40ish; a handy man with an axe and knew his job as a station hand. Greg was from the Cunnamulla Aboriginal camp, bright and helped Harry with his jobs. The manager, Gordon Simpson, was a kindly man, that spent most of the time in the office or just driving around in the Falcon ute. All in all, everything was going well, the jobs were completed on time and well done. The food was good and we all got on well together.

Social life also was great. I teamed up with the overseer, Ian, from Heywood station and went to town once every three weeks or so, meeting likeminded jackaroos, overseers and young managers. Nothing was communicated but we all seemed to gravitate at the same time whenever an event was on, like the Cunnamulla Show, races, rodeo, which I always participated in, dances, parties and the very popular Slim Dusty Show.

The Slim Dusty show was great. All the Aboriginals from miles around had Slim's records and they came where all the front seats in the marquee were reserved for them. The show was full of laughter and song with a lot of variety acts. And after being thoroughly entertained, we all tumbled out at interval time for drinks, ice-creams, chips and sweets. What amazed me was the hard-working entertainers were now the ones serving us our refreshments. We all loved the Slim Dusty Show.

Nancy was a slim, attractive teenager, well dressed, well spoken, who lived with her mum. Whenever something was on: a dance, ball, party, if you were the first of us bush blokes into town and invited her out, she would be pleased to go out with you, but if one of the other chaps got there first, you had to find someone else or go as a single. Her mum always welcomed us with tea and cake, had a chat asking what we did and what we were up to. She was a surrogate mother to us bushies. But it must be made clear that Nancy did not tolerate any 'funny' business and we all appreciated and respected her.

Another girl I just happened to sit next to at the pictures, asked me if I would escort her home at interval, as she had broken her shoe heel and had sore feet. Being the gentleman that I am, I said I would. On the way to her place, there must have been an event that had just finished and a man beside a big barbeque asked us if we wanted the left-over onions and garlic sausage. I refused, she accepted and he emptied them into a paper bag, glad to get rid of the scraps. Now Doreen, that was her name, had straight mousy hair, was slim with acne and she needed more than getting rid of pimples to make her attractive. As we came to her empty house, she produced the key to open the door, then threw the now empty bag of garlic sausage and onion fried rings into her garden after doing the fourth loud burp of the evening. She said, "Come in, I won't be long."

You know what's going to happen, Jack. You're in it up to your neck again.

She asked if I could play the piano that was there. I said I couldn't. She said, "I won't be long now."

I thought, *It doesn't take that long to find a shoe.* Then she appeared, not in jeans, a blouse and cardigan, but, well, I wasn't sure. Was it the sack dress they were talking about or a nighty? It was a bit sheer. She said, "Come into my bedroom, I've something to show you, that you might like."

Now, thoughts and voices were going full tilt in my head. A. Go for it, son, ya need it. B. Don't be silly, if anything is like her cake hole and breath, yer better run for it before you're poisoned.

Have you ever had sentences muddle up in your brain? You want to say something sensible, but another sentence jumps in and tangles things up and what comes out of your mouth is the last thing you want to happen. In my confusion, I replied to her, "I'm having a penis attack."

She said, "That's good, we better hurry then."

"No, no. I meant I'm having a gastric attack and I'm going to be sick." I rushed out the door, holding my stomach and pretending to vomit. I walked back to the theatre and decided, instead, to go back to the station where it was a safe place.

Another girl I was quite fond of, had won the Girl in a Million Quest. She owned a shop with her brother in Cunnamulla. We were both keen on each other; her brother offered me a partnership in his new barbwire business, but I declined as I thought there is enough barb wire sold now, why make more? Silly me, should have researched the operation. He ended up being a multi-millionaire in that business. The girl and I, as in the way of things, soon parted as good friends.

But at last, I had a true, loving and devoted partner. She was young, impetuous, lots of fun and we were in love at first sight. The boss had introduced her to me. Her name was Skipper, a pure-bred collie working sheep dog. We trained each other and we both learnt our lessons well. We became an excellent working team.

It was the winter in 1964, I came down with a bad flu, so did the boss, so did the community and the country. Schools were closed, businesses had no staff, babies and old people were dying. Everything came to a standstill that winter. But I survived as others did: the shearing, the stock work, the maintenance and the bore drains were cleaned. We did the work. The big boss regularly flew in a tiny plane or drove from Toowoomba to the property to see if everything was running properly. He gave me a bit of a compliment one day, and said, "Jack, you could be the manager of this place one day. I have noticed your work, keep it up."

Good things, however, came to an end. One night, as on

other nights, Robert, Greg and I would try strength contests on each other. Can you do this? What happens if two snakes eat each other, head to tail, at the same rate? What is left? They were fun contests with each other.

On this particular night, on the veranda of the shearers' quarters, we placed a small table in the middle and then we placed a pile of the shearers' mattresses at one end of the table. Then we would run up to the table, fly over it and somersault on to the mattress. How far could we fly? A chair was then put beside the table and we flew over that too and so it went on, until there was a massive run up over six chairs and a table which we managed to fly over and go further.

I don't remember the outcome, but I do remember when we put the furniture and mattresses back, we noticed we had broken three of the bearers under the veranda. We got up early the next morning and jacked the bearers up with blocks, so the veranda was level again. Being in charge, I thought it was my duty to tell Mr Simpson what had happened and that we had blocked up the broken bearers and would repair them on the weekend. He said not to worry about it as the veranda was so old and in decay.

At the end of the month, I noticed that $70 had been taken out of my pay. I asked, "Why is this?"

Mr Simpson replied, "To pay for the damage you did to the veranda."

I said, "We were prepared to fix it properly and you said not to worry about it. What's more, you cannot deduct a man's wages, it's not legal."

"I will decide if its legal or not, now get on with your work."

"I am sorry, but if you don't reimburse me my $70 right now, I will give notice to come into effect immediately."

He didn't answer, so I turned and went back to the quarters and told them what happened. Robert and Greg both said they were just as much to blame and if I was leaving now, so were they.

I packed up the ute with my gear and dog, went to see Mrs Simpson to thank her for her good cooking, but told her the three of us were leaving now.

"Oh dear, what has Gordon done now?"

"Sorry, but the men and I won't stand anyone interfering with our wages. I'm sorry, but that's the way it's turned out." I walked out of the kitchen, met the boys and we went on our way. In another time, I returned to Ardglen, but that is a different story.

On my way to Cunnamulla, I called in to Clevelane Station to see Larry and Bess Maunder. We often stopped there to see Larry, who was a real character. His wife, Bess, had two little girls. She was a great mother and a very intelligent woman. There was one problem, Larry was an alcoholic and nearly always inebriated. But it was fun to hear his stories. He had been an instructor in Tiger Moth and Wirraway aircraft during the Second World War. He was very frustrated as he wanted to fight in the war. I guess he was such a good instructor that they had kept him here in Australia. He used to tell us about training kids who eventually would be killed or seriously injured. This had played on his mind.

One of the many stories he told, was in the Tiger Moth, where the student was in the front of the aircraft and the instructor in the rear of the two-seater plane. There were two joy sticks to control the aircraft, one for the instructor and one for the student. When Larry thought the student was confident enough, he would throw his joystick away and say, "You're on your own now," but he always kept a spare under his seat, so the student would have to fly and land the plane on his own. That was the story Larry told me.

But someone else finished the story. It was my sister's late second husband, Laurie Stinson, who was a famous pilot in World War Two. He was trained by Larry and knew about the way Larry used to throw the joystick out but always kept a spare under his seat. The story went, Laurie removed the spare joystick from under Larry's seat and put it under his seat in the student cockpit. Off they went on their training flight. Larry felt his student was going well and told that to the student and threw his joystick out. Laurie, pretending he didn't hear, yelled back, "Is that what you want me to do?" and threw his joystick out too.

Well, panic ensued as Larry could not find his spare joystick and now the aircraft was uncontrollable! After Larry was given a well-deserved fright, Laurie put his spare joystick back in its holder, finished the exercise and landed safely.

This story told by these two men to me, could be just an old Airforce yarn, but I believe it was true, as the participants telling the story seemed genuine. It was at least 20 years between the telling of the two stories.

Larry gave me a job at $40 a week, good room, good tucker and I had to keep busy looking for worthwhile jobs. I decided to tidy/clean out the sheds. Everything was in a mess, no order and to find something took hours. Under one of the benches were four crates and a crystal-like substance leaking out of the boxes. I moved them to one side and found something to prise one of the crates open to see what was inside.

I'd had no experience with explosives, but I thought they might have been sticks of gelignite or dynamite, so I went to see Larry about them. He said, "I had forgotten about them. They have been there for years. You didn't see anything leaking from those boxes, did you?"

"Yes," I said, "there was this sorta crystal stuff leaking out."

"Don't tell me you moved them. If you did, we could have all been blown to smithereens. That liquid stuff is nitro-glycerine.

It's so unstable, it could go off at the slightest movement. I will look after that stuff on the weekend."

He did and blew it all up in the far paddock. The neighbours from miles around thought an earthquake had happened: windows were broken, things fell of shelves, inquiries were made, it all seemed a mystery. I don't know how he did it but whatever happened, he survived.

Larry lost his pilot's licence. The Tiger Moth was still on the property, but the goats had eaten half a wing. He lost it due to a stunt he performed, to frighten a man he disliked who was a patient at the Cunnamulla hospital. He flew the aircraft so low that the landing wheels ran along the corrugations of the hospital's roof, making a terrible din. It shook the building and all who were residing in it, were terrified.

The mulga tree is a great piece of vegetation. It has all the nutrients in it, but it lacks calcium. If they eat it, sheep need plenty of water or they bind up with sticks and leaves in their gut. It's also poisonous if you get a splinter or stake in any part of the body, as it releases a toxin into the bone. I know this from personal experience.

I had a mulga splinter. I didn't worry too much, until my right hand started to swell. I tried to get the splinter out, but it was in too deep. I thought, like all splinters, it would eventually work its way out or go round the blood system and stab me in the heart. But none of these things happened.

My hand was swollen, so swollen, it was a web infection that reached as far as the last joint in my fingers. The hand was so heavy, I had to wear a sling to hold it up. Hospital for you, young man, and so it was. The infection was so bad that I had to wait for the flying surgeon to come the following Thursday. Amputation of my right hand, they said. Oh my God, I will end up with a hook like a pirate for a hand. That would not be good.

Eight days in Cunnamulla hospital, with a very painful right hand. I think I was getting penicillin injections every day. The ward had six men in it, including myself. It was very hot as it was early December and the fans on the ceiling did not help much. The flies were very curious about us sick mortals. I used to watch the old man opposite me; he sat right on the edge of the bed with his head down looking at the floor, maybe for an hour, maybe more, then he would look up and inform everyone and no one in particular, that there were 192 flies on the floor beside his bed. Another day, the wardsman, with a covered body on a trolley, wheeled past us, he said, "A pity a few more of you bastards didn't die, I get an extra dollar for doing this."

The operating theatre was ready and the surgeon had just arrived.

"Quick Sir, there is a woman haemorrhaging badly."

There were staff running about, a big emergency. I was waiting for my terrifying turn for hours. The poor woman died. She had already had six kids and was told never to get pregnant again as there would be complications. As it turns out, that's what happened.

But what about me and my right hand?

"I'm so sorry," said the sister, "but we have had an emergency that took all the surgeon's time and he now must fly to Charleville for surgery waiting for him there. You will have to stay another week and hope with the drugs we are giving you, the infection will settle down."

And so it did, but that last week was very uncomfortable for us in the ward, as the poor woman who had died seven days ago, wasn't to be buried until the relations from Melbourne had viewed the body. The problem was, there was no cold room at the hospital and it was extremely hot, with millions of flies in that month of December. The only place for a body, at that time, was a gauzed hut at the back of our ward. Normally, they would bury a body as soon as possible. That is where they laid the poor woman. The stench from that gauzed hut, filtered into our ward, which was so overpowering that we had handkerchiefs over our noses, or hid under the sheets.

As the days wore on, the stink got worse. The flies and the heat made the decomposing body a terrible sight to see. The howls and screams and unrestrained crying from the relations when they came, haunted us for nights on end. It was horrendous.

I learnt a lot from Larry; he was a good teacher and he always made a joke, so I would remember what he was imparting to me. For example, during a mechanical class for a group of W.A.C. (Women Army Corps) the instructor asked the class how you would fix a large crack in a piece of metal, such as a mud guard on an army vehicle. No one could answer the question. The instructor explained that if you make or drill a hole just above the crack it will cease further expanding. A young blonde woman started giggling.

"Corporal, what do you see so funny about that?" he asked.

"Sir, I just realised what my belly button was for," she replied.

Larry taught me all about the safety of guns, making my own ammunition, the weights of projectiles and powder and the importance of clean water to all animals. In the terrible 64/65 drought, Larry had the best weight and quality of wool in the district, due to having clean bore water in every paddock and insisting the troughs be cleaned every fortnight. His sheep, like all the others in the district, was only on mulga for feed.

I said I would tell you about drinking water. An old Aboriginal caught me drinking from a tap up north in the Gulf country as I was thirsty. He said, "Boy, if you keep on drinking water when you feel thirsty, you will die. Only drink as much as you can at sunrise and then again at sunset or a little at rest."

Now, of course, this was against medical advice of the day because the body can't store water. I assumed the reason behind the Aboriginal's theory was that your body temperature is much hotter than the water you drink, therefore you sweat more, you lose salt and electrolytes and because of that you feel thirsty again. You drink more water and the whole cycle begins again. So much for the theory, but I practiced it and it's worked for me. When I was a kid, I never saw people walk around with bottles of water or drinking lots of the stuff. I learnt later the bushmen of Africa do the same, only drinking at sunrise and sunset.

Hell had broken loose. The wind was howling with rage, trees were bending in half, dust was swirling, iron was flapping on the roof and I couldn't see a thing. Larry yelled, "It's a cyclone. Women and children, seek shelter immediately. Jack, you climb up on the roof and nail it down."

I didn't think; I just did what I was told, which you did in my day, without question. I had the hammer and roofing nails and did the job safely. How I managed, I don't know. How did I hang on? Why wasn't I blown off? Why wasn't I hit by flying debris? Jack, really? Cyclone out at Cunnamulla? They only happen along the coast in north Queensland. Yea, that's right, but this one landed in Mornington Island and went inland, built up speed on its way back and wrecked the holiday places down the Gold Coast. It was January in 1964; it was called Little Audrey.

There was a disturbing side to Larry, due to his fondness of Amity Rum. Being an alcoholic, there were different moods: happy, depressed, sleepy, but when on Amity Rum, he was an abusive and violent man. Estell, the governess at the time, told me she always locked the door and put a chair under the doorknob and advised me to do the same. I said I couldn't as I had no door to my room. She said, "Jack, be extremely careful. When he gets the rum into him, anything can happen."

Estell left about two weeks after I arrived. Nothing to do with me; she became very frightened of Larry.

About alcohol, there were two other chaps who were alcoholics who owned blocks close to Ardglen. I won't mention their names as they were Rats of Tobruk and heroes. I enjoyed their company and stories. One of them used to order a carton of rum every week via the mail. His wife, after some time, got sick of this and his behaviour, so when the mailman came, she made sure she got to the rum before he did. And what did she do? She emptied the dozen bottles down the bore drain. Her husband, on hearing this, raced to the bore drain and, on his hands and knees, tried to drink as much as he could before it was all completely diluted.

I must mention, the women whose husbands suffered so much in all the wars, sheltered their children but lived with the nightmares and abuse. The ones who stayed to look after their husbands, through love and compassion, suffered, usually much longer than the wars themselves. I knew some of them and I dip my Akubra to all of them. Where are their medals of bravery?

This frightening Sunday, the little girls came running out of the house yelling, "Jack, Jack. Daddys going to shoot our dog."

It happened that the dog was barking and woke or annoyed the hungover Larry, so he got big Bertha, a double-barrel shot gun, ran out of the house and lined the shotgun up on the kid's puppy. The children were screaming, "Jack, save our puppy. Don't let him shoot it."

I said, "Come off it, Larry, you can't shoot the kids puppy because it was just barking."

He swung around with the gun pointing at me.

"I won't shoot the dog; I'll shoot you, you interfering bastard." He poked both barrels into my stomach, the hammers back and his drunken finger on the trigger. I was dead.

I was extremely calm. I remembered reading in some fiction book, that if someone holds a gun to your back and, if you are quick, you can deflect it before the brain tells the finger to pull the trigger and this is what I did. I said, looking Larry dead in the eye, "You wouldn't shoot me."

And at that, I swiped the barrels to my left. The gun fired. The force of me hitting the barrels away, stopped any powder or pellets landing on me. The gun was dropped. Then it was all over. I panicked, even though the gun was on the ground and the danger was over. I ran, so fast and so far, till I felt safe. I hid behind a bush; I was in shock; I vomited; I shook. I was a mess.

It was some time in the evening that I walked back to the homestead, thinking a lot. Previously, he had let loose with the shot gun at his nephew, who was fishing. He missed. He had threatened his wife with the gun, even held a bayonet to her throat, saying he would kill her, then said, "What's the use? You wouldn't suffer, so I'll kill the kids instead," and went into their bedroom with the bayonet, with Bess screaming.

There were other instances when he was on that particular rum. It made him mad and dangerous. Something terrible would happen sometime soon. It had to be stopped.

Larry always preached that you had to be sober on Monday mornings for a fresh start to the week. Monday, the next day after the event, I said to Larry, "We are short of supplies and rum, do you mind coming to town with me?"

"Only if we take the Nash Rambler." A great car that I was only too pleased to drive.

Getting a shopping list from Bess, we headed for town. As we neared the main drag I said to Larry, "I'm taking you to the police station. You tried to kill me yesterday and you have attempted to hurt your family. I'm sorry, I like you Larry, but I feel I must do this."

He replied calmly, "Don't take me to the police, take me to the doctors."

"No, I'm taking you to the police."

He pleaded with me and I relented and took him to the

doctors. I was in the waiting room when Dr Greg came out and said to me, "Larry has committed himself and I will arrange for him to go to the Gold Coast facility where he will be treated." And so, it was.

After I did the shopping, I drove back and told Bess what had happened. She was furious, no, hopping mad, abusing me, practically screaming at me. What right did I have to interfere with her family? Why didn't I discuss what I was going to do? And on it went. Then she walked away, doing the angry woman's walk.

She came back later after she calmed down, saying, "Jack, fill the Rambler up, help me pack it with the things I left on the veranda. We are leaving for our unit at the Gold Coast now, so we can be with Larry," adding more quietly, "You still had no right to do what you did, but I can understand why. Now you can care-take the place."

Quick work, Jack. Get rid of the boss and end up as station manager in six months. Alright, it actually was a caretaker's job, but what are titles?

I had plenty to do as the drought was getting a hold on and every day, I had to check the sheep. All the troughs at Clevelane were in the centre of the paddock. When sheep got hungry or thirsty, they walked around the fence line looking for feed or water. If they were unsuccessful, they would just camp in a corner and end up dying. I had to check for this, then moved them to the water in the middle of the paddock again. Maybe having a water supply near a fence line might have been a good management tool in a bad drought.

There was a cement block to be made for insulation of a big pump. I had to make sure all waters were clean and working, put out salt and calcium blocks and the chore every second day was to check the sheep got to their water supply in their paddocks. I had to feed myself, protect myself from all the brown snakes that emerged from the house yard, on the veranda, in the kitchen, on the steps, in the garden. Not ornery snakes but big two-metre killers. Having shot three with Big Bertha, I was rattled so high tailed it next door to Clestfrane Station and my friend, the manager, Cliff Pilcher.

We will meet Cliff in the far distant future. He could talk and talk, then talk some more, about his life in the outback, his New Guinea war stores, where he got shot, recovered and served again. Cliff sometimes helped me with moving the thirsty sheep and gave me help when I needed it. We would camp for lunch under a shady tree and, usually, it was too late in the day to do anything else as time slipped by very quickly when Cliff was telling yarns. He said not to worry about any more snakes as they had probably been living there for years, but were too frightened to come out, with all the noise Larry made, as well as the girls. Now it was quiet, they came to explore.

A few weeks had passed. Phil from Derain Station, a good friend of Larry and Bess, came over and said that their place was now on the market and the agents would send one of their men to get the property and all its contents ready for sale.

"Thanks Jack, for all you have done. I have a cheque and a letter from Bess for you," said Phil, "Would you believe, in such a short time, Larry has totally given up the drink and, more surprising, smoking? But he is not the same man, he is very subdued and quiet, but the main thing is that Bess, Larry and the girls are very happy with their new life down at the coast. Jack, no one will probably thank you for what you did. It made me feel guilty that I did not do what I knew I should have."

"Phil, do I have to leave on the spot?"

"The agent knows you're here and you can stay till you get another job, which I don't think will be too difficult for you at this time."

We shook hands. I did not know it then, as well as with Cliff, I would end up good friends with him and his wife in the distant future.

Jack at Lindfield Station Julia Creek 1963.

Lindfield Homestead Julia Creek 1963.

Ardglen Homestead Cunnamulla 1964.

Jack's quarters Wongermere on the Nebine, Bollon 1965.

Pig hunt at Wongermere. Jack is holding the pig on the left.

Jack riding at Cunnamulla Rodeo 1967.

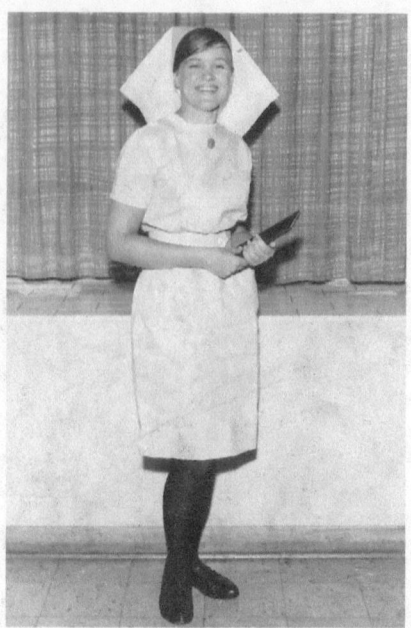

Helen graduating midwifery 1966.

Jack with Skipper the dog and young horse.

Jack and Helen's wedding, November 1967.

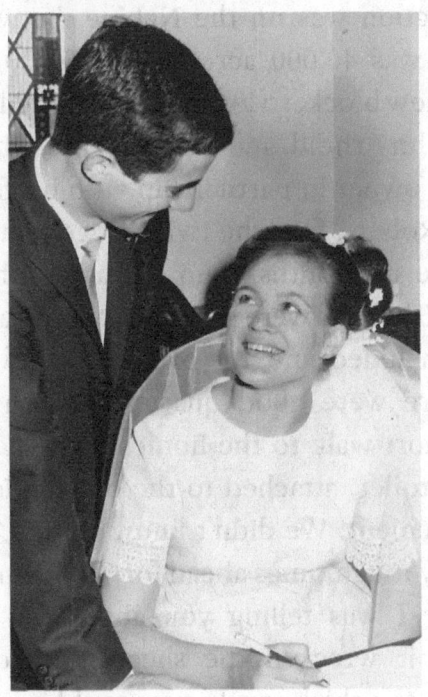

C.6

Wongamere, Melbourne again

A Life Changing Experience

Wongamere Station was on the Nebine, between Charleville and Bollon. It was 40,000 acres, with 10,000 sheep and 300 cattle. It was a new block, so lots of work needed to be done. The manager was John Arnold, and his wife, Jane, whose father, R.G. White, was the owner in partnership with his family. They had four children, Robert, five, the twins Roger, and Dudley, three years, and Susie six months. John was a great boss and Jane, a fabulous cook. The kids were fun, but very mischievous.

The staff included: me, the overseer, a governess and two jackeroos. There were good quarters, which just had been renovated, a short walk to the homestead. There was a men's bathroom and toilet, attached to the outside laundry. All was great and convenient. We didn't know it then, but there were going to be very tough times ahead for Wongamere.

Remember I was telling you about the cyclone, Little Audrey? Well, it wrecked the shearing shed and yards at Wongamere. In the thick scrub, you could come to a clearing where trees were flattened in a circle as if a huge twister had landed and taken off again to land and flatten another area. First jobs were, build new yards and shearing shed, as well as carrying on with the normal husbandry for the stock. Those jobs kept us all very busy. It was January and the feed was drying out. We were waiting for the rains to come but they were late.

It was decided by the people in the district to have a community centre at Boatman Station, which is 136km from Charleville, 118km from Morvan, 142km from Bollon and 209km from Cunnamulla, using a paddock beside the road to build it. A couple of tennis courts were made using the best surfacing of ant bed, which took a lot of crushing, watering and rolling, more watering and more rolling. All this took time with lots of local volunteers, which had only the weekends to work on the centre. John, my boss, made a huge screen as it was decided to have an open-air picture theatre as well, which left us making the projector box, also digging the holes for the canvas seats that could be easily taken off at the end of the show. It was a badly needed centre for the surrounding families to meet, have some recreation and forget the looming hard times that were coming.

It was the time of the station wagon and all the young families from roundabout had one. This night at the community centre, the pictures were being shown. Always, the first film was for the children, a mixture of cartoons and a Disney movie. After intermission, a more adult movie was shown. Now, during intermission, all the mums and dads would take their sleepy children to bed in the back of the station wagon, making sure they were safe and join the others for the feature film.

While the film was being shown, some rogues went and swapped all the sleeping children into the different station wagons. Now, all were tired after the movies and drove the hundreds of kilometres to their homes. When they arrived home, they picked up the sleeping children from the back of the car. They suddenly realised, they were holding the wrong child. Panic ensued. They started ringing up on party lines that became jammed, racing about in cars to hand a child to its rightful owner and to pick up their own darlings. No child was lost; most slept through the dramas of the parents, after time and a bit of anger. It was thought of as a great practical joke. What do you think?

The horror of country life became apparent as the drought took hold, The rains did not come, the dams were drying, the feed was gone, so were the employees as the owners didn't have the money to pay them or they did not like the rotten jobs they were asked to do. But the genuine managers and owners had to tough it out.

My daily job, of many, many months, would start at 5am, loading bags of calcium and salt blocks into the ute, then I'd drive to the paddocks, put the blocks out and the calcium into wooden troughs. On the way, I would see dozens of emus dead and hanging upside down with their legs twisted in the wire fence. Then, on to the one dam left, are you ready for it? Bogged sheep with their eyes pecked out and their bowels pecked around the anus. Then the culprits would pull their intestines out while the sheep were still alive.

I hated the crows. I would have to unbog the poor sheep, slit their throats and cart them away from the water, maybe half a dozen or more a day. The cute little lambs, waiting for their mother's milk, had to be euthanised as well. Then on to the tractor or dozer, whichever was working. The sheep were waiting for me, to push mulga to them for feed. The dust, the stench, the jerking of the machine as it pushed down mulga trees and bounced over the trunks. I needed a rest, a sandwich, a mug of tea, but how could I, when the sheep are so hungry that they have eaten all the feed you have pushed that morning? I would get home by 6pm, have dinner, feed the horses and dogs and go to bed at 9pm.

The boss was just as busy, carting water all day to put in the dam. Using the chainsaw to cut more feed. Repairing machinery that had broken down, mainly due to age and constant use. There was no money to replace them; we just had to make parts. The poor missus alone all day with four young children. No one to talk to, no one for comfort, looking out of the window, seeing all was dead.

If you will excuse me, it's not on the hit parade yet, but I made up a song on the tractor. The tune is just the noise of the droning engine. (See back pages)

Most nights, I just collapsed and went into an exhausted deep sleep. Other nights, I had dreams, some of me flying around my room or in a street. They were my favourite. I had ones of falling but not hitting the ground. Wasn't keen on them. I dreamt of a girl, which was rare for me. It was a haunting sort of a dream. The girl was walking down a street, wearing a brownish, woollen skirt with light squares on it and a pretty blouse. It wasn't what she was wearing that struck me, it was her face. It had an aura of happiness and love. It had to be some angel beckoning me to heaven. Another dream I had was getting lost in a building and could not find my way out. But best of all I had serial dreams. Where it would continue the next night and the next. I called them soapy dreams.

It all was so tough. Some property owners gave their station to the banks. I had a great friend, Peter, who was a jackaroo at a property not far from where I was working. Sometimes on a weekend off, we would drive to Charleville, have a session and meal at Hotel Corones and just have a relaxing time. He said his boss gave him some time off to see one of his parents, who was sick. That was his story. It was found out, Peter had incurable cancer. He came back to work and we had our trip to town. I asked about his sick parent, who eventually got better. Later that week, I was informed he had gassed himself in his VW as he didn't want to worry his parents about his cancer. It was just getting to me: the drought, all the killing, the dying, the hopelessness of it all. And it could all be solved by some good, soaking rain.

As the drought continued, I sometimes went to Charleville with the family, to help with supplies and the four children. This particular time, waiting for the Arnolds, I had nothing to do. It's funny, you always want to get to town and yet, it's boring and you can't wait to get home. With nothing to do, I went into a chemist shop and, just to fill in time, I asked about what the best contraceptives were.

Well, the chemist was pleased to expound all his knowledge on the subject, which was fine by me, as it helped fill in the time. But I sorta had to make a purchase in the end. Spermatozoon cream and a packet of condoms was in the white paper bag as I left the shop. Not long after, I saw the missus, who was only a few years older than me, with some shopping, two grizzling children and the twins causing trouble.

I helped with the parcels, while I had one crying kid on my arm and hanging on to the other. The missus held the twins; a lovely, domestic scene. It happened that the chemist I was talking to not so long ago, came out of his shop and walked down the street and saw me and the missus struggling with four, little, tired kids, as well as the shopping. As he passed, he gave me a wink and said, "You won't have any more problems now."

"What was that all about?" asked the missus.

I mumbled about something needing band aids for my blisters. A couple of years later, I told her the truth and she roared with laughter.

My constant companion and mate, Skipper, loved water. If he smelt water a mile away, he would leave me with the sheep and hightail it over there. When I arrived, he would be immersed in the water, giving me a joyful grin. The kids had a little paddle pool. If Skipper was around, he would decide the pool was his and frighten the children with his splashing and antics. He also loved the drying out water holes. Indeed, if it had water in or around, the dog would find it.

This day I had to cart water; this was in the big international truck with a 2000l tank on the back. We had to travel to next door's bore, some 10 kilometres away. Skip wanted to come for a ride, so I lifted him on the front of the tray body beside the water tank. Soon as we arrived at the flowing bore, Skipper saw water and jumped in. He didn't feel a thing. I did. As I lifted my mate from the near boiling water, the tears flowed. I lost me mate; it had happened again. I buried my companion beside his favourite water hole. I didn't function too well that week.

A fortnight later, the boss, one night, turned up to the quarters with a 12-month-old little, black and tan kelpie puppy, saying, "I think you need a friend," as he handed the dog to me.

She licked my face and wagged her tail. I held her close, saying thank you to the boss, who walked away to leave me to get acquainted with my new mate. You can never replace a mate that's passed, but you can always cultivate a new friend. Her name was Prue.

We, the surrounding community, were thankful for the Parrs of Aqua Downs holding a non-denominal service monthly, with of course, the ladies brought their best creations for supper, as indeed they did for picture night. The minister was great. He understood the pain, suffering and hardship of his congregation. He picked good hymns that reflected hope and love, with catchy tunes that we all loved to sing. He didn't push so much hard religion but was more about helping each other with kindness and love. One night, we were all deep in prayer, when a 'psst', a whisper was heard.

"The horses are in the garden."

The solemn prayer to God for rain was upheld, as everyone,

including the minister, scrambled out of their chairs to chase the horses out and save Mrs Parr's garden.

A bachelor and spinster ball was advertised at Bollon and the six of us had to go: Peter and Beryl, George and Margo, me and Elizabeth; all good mates but nothing serious going on between the six of us.

We hired a room at the Bollon Hotel for the girls to get changed into their finery and us blokes to smarten up, as travelling hundreds of miles on rough dirt roads, one seems to get a bit dusty during the trip. We had just the most fabulous time: great band, great company. We danced, we drank, we ate, we talked, we laughed, life was good.

About 3am, we decided enough of a good time was enough. We went back to the hotel to get our gear and, there and then, it was decided, by unanimous decision, that we were too tired to drive home and might as well stay at the hotel. We pushed the two single beds together, took our shoes off and all squeezed into the two single beds, still wearing all our best clothes.

There was a knock on the door at 6.30am. Someone said, "Yes?" and an old lady with a tray of tea came in.

She looked at six of us jammed into two single beds, with just a half sheet over us and said, with a shocked expression, "I hope you will all be at the Bachelor and Spinsters Ball next year." She put the tray down on the dresser and scurried out, shutting the door behind her.

John, my boss, was an extraordinary man. An unqualified engineer, he could repair or make anything: a shearing shed out of railway line, even the trusses. Anything mechanical, he could fix, repair, make parts for. An example was, I flew over a cattle grid in my car, but the other side of the grid was washed away. Therefore, as I reached the other side, the car nosedived into the dirt, wrecking the whole front suspension. After getting the car home, the boss dismantled it all, straightened and then plated it with heavy steel plate from the wrecked Bren Gun carrier that was in bits at the junk heap. After the repairs, with only a ruler and level, he did the toe in and adjustments. The car drove better than it ever did before. A lot of miles were safely completed after the repair. The boss had one problem; he used to say he could do anything. The annoying thing was that he could and proved it many times.

He taught me how to pull an engine down and rebuild it. He showed me the tools and how to use them. He taught me welding, electric and gas and how to build things. Something a chap without a father sometimes lacks. I'm indebted to John Arnold as my teacher.

We had to cement the woolshed floor. We drove to Charleville to get supplies and, on the way, we found a good shovel on the side of the road. We picked it up and continued on to town. On the way back, we saw a figure walking along the road. The boss said, "We found a shovel, now we have found someone to use it."

As we got closer to the figure, we were surprised to see a young Aboriginal only in shorts, carrying something in a bit of rag. Boss said, "Ask him if he wants a job. If he says yes, he is your responsibility and you look after him."

We pulled up beside him. I said, "G'day, you want a job? I have to make a cement floor for a woolshed and I need someone to help me. Pay is basic wage, full tucker and board." He raised his hand for the car door handle and mumbled, "Okay," as he got in the ute. We made room for him.

Cliff was his name. When we picked him up, he was walking from Charleville to Bollon, a distance of 263km. In the bit of rag he was carrying a half loaf of bread. With no rain that year, we knew of no water on his route. Incredible.

Don't know if he was a full blood or not, but he would have been pretty close to it. His English was not good but after a while,

I managed to understand him and he with me. He camped with me in my quarters and would not eat with us, which was normal, so the missus always made extra when doing our meals and I would take his meal up to him.

We both worked hard, shovelling the sand, gravel and cement into the mixer, then when ready, pouring it out on the new floor. We took turns making the cement and helped the boss lay the cement to make the wool room floor.

We got on well together. I helped him start a bank account so he could save enough to make a hut for himself. That is what he wanted more than anything. He taught me a bit about tracking and survival ways. I told him stories in the book I was reading. Cliff was always very clean, showering every night. We all pooled and bought him some working clothes and boots for when he was cementing, which he hardly wore. I could not help it after a month of holding my mouth, I had to say, "Cliff, you stink. Your smell has impregnated the quarters."

"What do I smell like?" asked a shocked Cliff.

"Like decaying eucalypt leaves in a drying out water hole," I said.

Then Cliff shocked me by saying, "You fella stink pretty big yourself."

"What, me stink? What do I stink like?"

"Your stink is sweet and sickly. Make me want to vomit every night."

Gosh, I had no idea my smell was causing him trouble and it told me what a polite fella he was, not saying anything and putting up with my stink. When I was so rude to criticise his natural smell.

One day, about three months later, I couldn't find Cliff. After some searching, I asked the missus if she had seen him. She had as she had let him ring up a taxi to Cunnamulla. I rang the Commonwealth bank manager and asked if Cliff had come in and drawn some money out. He told me, not some, but all of it.

"You mean, the whole balance of nearly $500?"

"No, it was $648 he drew out and closed the account. I rang the cops to warn them," said the bank manager, "It's ok Jack, the whole camp has started already and we are keeping a very close eye on it."

All he wanted was a hut, but his instincts made him give a party to his family and all his friends. It's nice to be friendly and helpful, it's their way. I missed Cliff, but not his odour. I couldn't get used to it.

We had some two inches of rain after 12 months of nothing; the boss and family had a break. I spent Christmas alone looking after everything. I was promised a month off when they came back after their three-week holiday. The rain did not break the drought but gave a bit of relief and showed that there was such a thing called rain.

I had told Mum I'd be home for Christmas a few months ago. I had to revise it to January. Soon as the family arrived, I took off for Melbourne. Gosh, why didn't I go for a good holiday to the Gold Coast or somewhere? I had earned it, but Melbourne it was. I hadn't seen the family for two years and felt obligated to go. *Good on you Jack, always doing the right thing except doing something for yourself.*

I drove down to Melbourne in my two-tone, grey and pink, EH Holden station wagon, the ones with fins on the back. Going through the south of New South Wales, I saw police everywhere on the road, up trees and hiding in bushes. What was going on? I was pulled up a few times, asked where I was going and having a good look in the car, then telling me to move on, without an explanation.

Later, I was pulled up again. The same questions, the good look in the car, at last an explanation.

"Where you staying the night?" the senior constable asked.

"I got my swag; I'll camp off the road somewhere."

"You take some very sound advice, stay the night in a motel. I see you have a gun there and some clothes. Guess you are going on holidays; you would have a bit of cash on you as well?"

"So what?"

"An escaped prisoner from Pentridge Goal, who has shot and killed a prison guard, is on the loose and we expect he's on his way, today or tonight, to pass this way on the way to Sydney. You would be the ideal person for him to come across and be robbed, taking your car, gun, money and personal effects. So, for your own safety, stay in a motel for the night."

Gee, an escaped murderer on the run. I wondered if there is a huge reward out for his capture. I drove on thinking how I could catch him, be a hero and get rich.

It was getting dark. I saw a bit of a track leading off the main road, so I took it and found myself a nice camp site in a sheltered spot in amongst some bushes and trees. I put out my swag, loaded my gun, made a small fire, cooked some baked beans and a quart of tea. And went to bed.

I could tell you that later that night, I was disturbed by a slow-moving car coming in my direction. I jumped out of my swag and hid behind a large gum tree with my .243 rifle cocked. The car slowed and stopped a few metres from my car, a man got out. I stepped out behind the tree, pointing the gun at him.

"Lie down on yer stomach with your arms behind your back, one slight move and your dead." He didn't have a chance. I bundled him into my car and drove to the nearest police station.

Well, it could have happened like that. Nothing disturbed me that night. I continued on my journey to Melbourne. One day I did catch a murderer; I'll tell you about that later.

The radio and papers were full of this escaped prisoner, Ronald Ryan, and it was expected he had travelled to Sydney. It was a ruse; they caught him in suburban Melbourne a few days later. They hung him the following year, the last man to be hung in Australia.

It was good to see Mum and Gran. *I've seen them, might as well head back to Queensland*, I thought. No way, I had to see my sister with the new baby. I looked at my first nephew but he did not impress me much. I mean, all babies looked the same to me. Baby foals, calves or lambs, even joeys all look cute, but babies?! My sister encouraged me to pick him up. I did so to please her but handed him back a few seconds later. I did a quick trip up to Orbost to see my father, who had gone bankrupt and was working as a salesman in the country clothing store. It was good to see a man in his 60s still earning a living and trying to secure a job as a share farmer, which he eventually did.

I knew there was trouble as soon as I saw her. It was Karla, the sister of the boy I used to muck about with. We went to the same grammar school, except he was two years my senior but we were in the same scout group. They lived the next street to ours.

"I'm so pleased you're down from Queensland; you must come to my 21st birthday party next Saturday. Pleeeease," she begged.

"What, 21 already? Gee, what are you doing with yourself?" I replied.

"I'm a nursing student at the Royal Melbourne Hospital. I can tell you all about it later, but you will come to my party? It would be important to me that you be there."

"I don't know, I'm not good at parties, or girls for that matter and I must go back to Queensland at the end of next week, so thank you for asking but…"

"No buts, you're coming and that's the end of this conversation," and off she went up the hill to her place.

I told Mum about the invitation, and she said I should go.

"Mum I'm not interested. It will be all highfalutin' city

people. I would be like a fish out of water and the only person I would know is Karla's family. And anyway, I wouldn't have a clue what to wear."

"I think you should go; the family has been good to you; I suggest you have a long hard think about going."

I know there were discussions between Karla's mum, Mrs Thwaites, and my mum. A few days later, there appeared on my bed, a new smart shirt, tie, socks and underwear. My best sports coat and slacks, that I bought two years ago and had never worn, were also on my bed, nicely dry cleaned.

"Hey Mum, you giving clothes away to the salvos?" I cheekily teased.

"I think you will be wearing them in a couple of days," was her answer.

I gave in, showered and dressed, feeling all tight and uncomfortable and wrapped up like an Egyptian mummy, as I left to drive the one kilometre to the party. I said to my mother, "I will be back in 10."

I was right, they were all pale students, either medical or law. The girls were the same. I was well out of my element. Karla rushed up to me, grabbed my hand and introduced me to all, saying this is my best friend from outback Queensland. A shake of the hand, a smile and they went back talking to their friends. I was working out how I could leave diplomatically, when I saw this girl come round the corner holding the hand of Karla's little sister. She wore a navy tailored dress. She looked up and I could not believe it, the aura of happiness and love in her features, the smile, the dimples in her cheek, the kissable lips. This was the angel that I had dreamt about six months ago. It couldn't be true. I knew without any doubt that this was my future wife, forever.

She let go of the little girl's hand and walked up to me, saying in a sing song voice, "You must be Jack. I'm Helen., Karla has told me so much about you."

We were the last to leave the party. We somehow belonged and seemed to morph together. We knew each other, no awkward moments. For the first time in my life, I felt complete. We just danced and talked; we didn't notice anyone; our eyes were glued to each other.

"Excuse me, you two, it's getting late, everyone has gone. Are you taking Helen home?" asked Karla.

"Oh yes, I'd love to."

I took Helen to the Royal Melbourne Hospital nurses' quarters where she was in her final year and parked outside. We talked a little bit. She told me she was 22 years old and her father owned a dairy farm at Inverloch. The talking stopped. The kissing and cuddling began. Helen would pause the pash, to say 'hi', to nurses going off and on duty, which was a bit embarrassing. Then she mentioned that off-duty nurses were not allowed back in the quarters till 6am. I thought it a bit of a con but I didn't mind as the activities in my wagon were, surprisingly, pleasant and bloody wonderful.

Later that morning my mother had to say, "I saw you sneaking into your room at 7am. You told me you would be only away for 10 minutes. Guess you enjoyed the party?"

I was getting desperate. I rang the nurses' quarters twice a day, but she was unavailable or on duty but at last she answered the phone. I asked her out for a date. She asked, "Where are we going?"

I didn't have a clue. I said, "It's a surprise."

She said, "What should I wear?"

I said, "Your best," then arranged to pick her up on Wednesday at 6.30pm.

"Mum I'm in trouble." I told her about the conversation.

"Where am I going to take her? And I said, wear your best. What if I pick her up in a ball gown bedecked with jewellery and a bloody tiara, I'm cooked."

"No dear, I don't think there are any balls at the moment. There is, though, a very posh restaurant just opened called, Top of The Town. I suggest you make a reservation." And so, I did.

She was radiant and beautiful, with her long, fair hair done up in a French roll. She wore a halter dress, going under her arms, exposing her shoulders, with a wide collar. The material was satin with a colourful patten of 20 cent size circles. She had made the dress herself and it was beautifully tailored.

We had a fabulous time, working on the menu and wine. Helen ordered a flounder; I ordered a fillet mignon, The fillet mignon was a small meal, but poor Helen was embarrassed with a huge silver platter with a whole flounder on it. But we both laughed, enjoying a white sparkling wine with our meal. We managed one more date before I headed back to Queensland.

When I headed back to the bush, I was sad and felt lost. Helen knew I was leaving early at 4am and watched at the nurses' quarters window, hoping for a glimpse of my car as I passed the hospital on my way. She said she felt as I did, sad and lost.

It was back to the dust, the drought and the starving animals. There was no sign of goodness from the couple of inches of rain that had fallen a month ago. We were still heavily in drought. But there was a difference. The boss caught me swooning, holding on to a tree. As he passed, he said, "Boy, you have got it bad. I hope she is worth it."

I did not answer, there was nothing to answer to. But I kept seeing her face, hearing her voice. I yelled into space, "I love you!" and I did. Can you believe three meetings with Helen and I felt secure?

The letters started. I wrote a few without any answer, which caused me some concern, so I threatened to send a stuffed snake, if I didn't receive one soon.

We wrote and, to this day, we still have all our letters. We had both saved them as if they were the thread that held us together. They were not romantic, with a lot of mushy stuff, just about our lives. Please find below two of our first letters to each other.

Cape Patterson Rd.
Inverloch
13-3-66

Dear Jack,
I've been meaning to write this over the last few days but just didn't seem to be able to fit it in. However, I've got a few spare minutes now and shall do my best to get it finished.

*I'm on holidays at the moment and well overdue at that. That's my home address on top. Do you know what I did last Sunday night? I was at a twenty-first (wasn't as good as Karl's) and I fell down a couple of stairs. Wasn't very bright of me, was it? Anyway, on Monday I could hardly walk so I hobbled up to the doctor's, and he sent me for an x-ray, because he thought it (my leg) may have been broken, but after spending half the morning in x-ray and the other half in the nurse's sick bay, they decided it **was** only sprained, so I have been hobbling around on one foot over the past week. At least I get a seat on the trams.*

What made me furious was the fact that I had some driving lessons and couldn't push the clutch in. it would be about better by now, but I went and rounded in the cows for Dad the other night and, for some reason, cows just don't stick together and there was one in every corner of the paddock. So, you can picture "Helley" hobbling from one corner to the other. Fortunately, our paddocks are much smaller than yours.

There I was "Caaaarunning" or "Don't just stand there you silly thing, move" because they don't move till you get right behind them and give them a wack on the rump. Took me about an hour to get 70 cows half a mile, (Don't laugh.) I would have saddled the horse. But I wasn't sure how you did it. You'll have to teach me how one day.

Let me tell you about our holidays. My father and I are leaving for Tasmania tomorrow by air because Dad doesn't know what kind of sailor he is. Poor old Dad, he hasn't had a holiday for several years and I just about had to twist his arm up his back to get him to go away for a holiday. "Who wants to go away for a holiday?" Anyway, I had one back in September, two days mind you. The last 12 months have been a big strain on Dad. At the beginning of last year, my mother became ill and was so till June last year, when we lost her, which was a blow to all of us. Let's change the subject.

Guess what? Karla was looking through the professional list in the "Age" and she found a job for me. Have a guess where it was, in fact two guesses. I never thought would have guessed, but you are right! Cunnamulla. And the way I felt at the time I would have packed up and gone.

What's the big idea of thinking I wouldn't write to you? Really, but I would like a stuffed snake. Mrs Thwaites and Karla are dying to see it. Every time I go out to the Thwaites, all I get from the whole family, mind you, is: How's the stuffed snake?

Anyway, thank you for your very amusing and informing letter, just what I need after a hard day's work.

John Alexander, what's this tall story about the Abos getting hungry? They wouldn't eat me I'm too tough, besides they would only have to look at me and they would run. I can't think of any more news so will say by now, to the fella from Cunnamulla.

Love,
Helen
ps. shall send you a card from Tassie.

Jack's answering letter follows:

Wongamere Stn.

Morven Qld.
21-3-66

Dear Helen,

It was good to hear from you. Thanks for your letter. I hope we are not going to have a competition on writing the longest letter, because I can see in the not-too-distant future, that I will be sending a whole writing pad of this and that.

I am pretty buggered tonight as we were up at 3.30 this morning mustering twelve ~~thousand~~ hundred (getting carried away) sheep and jetting them for blowfly, err, in case it rains.

Well, we have just come home from the yards eight miles away and I have just showered and waiting for the dinner bell to go. I might have told you before that I take about four days to finish a letter that I write to you. I only have from knock-off time till seven to write; the time now is quarter to seven. The reason is that tea is at seven and after tea, the insects are so bad you can only hide under the mosquito net and the lights (generator) goes off at nine, so I go to bed and sleep and, mind you, I'm really ready for it. Of course, I would go to bed soooo much earlier if I had, err, your company.

You were a silly billy to fall down those steps, (you weren't tipsy, were you?) Anyway, I hope all is well now. You might not believe me but on the sixth, which I guess is the same day you had your mishap... (Oh, excuse me there goes the bell, I better go.)

Today is Wednesday. We mustered and jetted sheep yesterday and the pump broke down. I was a couple of hours fixing it and did not get home until 7.30. So, I was very tired and afraid I couldn't write another page to Helly so I shall have to write three tonight.

Now I was about to tell you what happened to me on Sunday the 6th. On that day I went water skiing on the Warrego River and, oh I came to grief. It happened like this: I was trying to be clever with a single ski. Anyway, we were turning around to come back to *the ramp when I pulled the tow rope back too much and, instead of doing a nice turn on the river, I ended up skiing a short distance on the riverbank which came to a halt due to a Coolabah tree. What happened? Just a sore knee, big bump and bruise and a very, very sore thumb. So, I was hopping along like a tailless kangaroo for a few days. We were in the same boat that week, but I think you may have been worst off.*

Did you get your driver's licence? Show you how to saddle a horse, I'm sure you know how to. I prefer riding bare back for short rides, but a saddle thankyou when I'm riding all day. Please excuse me, the bell again.

Well, here I am again, I did not do much today. It was a sort of odd job day, but tomorrow it will be mustering and jetting again. The two jackaroos gave notice this week to finish at the end of the month. I asked the boss if he was going to get some more, but he said he couldn't, because of the severity of the drought, he had to look after the station's finances. So, it looks like we have to slug it out ourselves.

My dear girl, how on earth did you fit all that stuff in the station wagon for your and Karla's marvellous trip around the Snowy? I would think by the sounds of it, you would need a two-ton truck. My, you are doing things in style. I must say there is no Burke and Wills about you two. I hope you have a good time. But I wish I could be a fly on the wall, you know, see what you get up to and watch you jump as I tickle your face at night. (Being a fly of course).

So, you would like a stuffed snake? Well, I will see what I can do, you may have to wait though.

I went to the "Mulla" last weekend and had my first experience with Dollar and Cents. Hell, what a muddle, I'm sure I was rooked left right and centre. I didn't do much in town, a bit of shopping, a small session at the pub, the flicks at night and a good greasy meal at the Creek café.

There are a few rodeos coming soon so I will see if I can ride the outlaws a bit better this year.

Believe it or not, I think I have finished, run out of gossip. What we should do is send each other a tape. Now have I anymore to say? Nope, that's about it. Hope to hear from you again soon.

Love Jack

ps. What does B stand for in your initials?

That was typical of the letters we both sent to each other for the next two years. Please respect them, they are very private and personal letters, so they are for your eyes only.

Helen graduated with Honors as a registered nurse, then moved to Sydney to train as a midwife at the King George Hospital. She and a few of her graduating friends moved into a house at Newtown, close to the hospital.

Meanwhile I was pushing mulga for feed, yes, and carting water and all the many little jobs that came up regularly. Midyear with cooler weather and some much-needed rain, the boss gave me a break of seven days. I did work long hours sometimes. On weekends, I didn't ever get overtime wages, in fact, money was short. Even my wages cheque bounced once, but all was made good, so a break on full pay was a reward.

I flew down in a Friendship Fokker, which was a weekly service from Cunnamulla to Sydney, stopping at major towns on the way. I was the only one on the plane from Cunnamulla, so the hostess asked if I would like to go up the front. I went and talked to the two pilots when the captain said, "Would you like to have a go at flying?"

"Bloody oath," I said.

He got out of his seat and here I was, in the captain's seat, flying a Friendship Fokker aircraft. With instructions, I flew straight and level and did some slight turns. I'm sure the co-pilot was using the rudders and ready to take over quickly, but it was great. The aircraft responded so well to the controls. The thrill didn't last long as the captain said, "We are coming into Dubbo to pick up some passengers, so back to your seat young fella and buckle up."

"Gee thanks for giving me a go. I want to learn to fly now, it was great."

The rest of the plane trip was boring. I hired a small Austin car to visit the girl I had dreamed of for the last six months. She was more wonderful than I had imagined, even with her dull midwife's uniform with black stockings. We dined and went for walks and drives, between Helen's nursing shifts. A nice drive to the Blue Mountains looking down at the beautiful views, then dropping her off at her residence while I continued to my cheap hotel in the city. Could I have stayed with Helen? Talked about it, but with five nurses going on and off shifts and little furniture, there wasn't an option.

Back at Wongamere, pushing scrub, losing sheep, hearing sheep were selling for 10 cents a dozen, things were getting bad. Huge dust storms came rolling in from the west. They were so thick I could hardly breathe, even with a hanky over my nose. I honestly felt the dozer start to climb the dust wall; it was so thick. Then we would get terrifying storms.

I was out at the back paddock some 11km from the homestead, checking some cattle, when from blue sky came a nasty storm. We, the horse and I, had just started for home when it hit. The lightning flashed and exploded all around us. It was dangerous fork lightning, spearing darts everywhere. The horse and I were terrified. He, because his instincts told him he was in grave danger. My fear was the iron bit and stirrups, the sweating horse and my height in the saddle. All prime targets for a lightning strike. The horrendous claps of thunder, like two empty iron water tanks clashing together. Wind came with a force of a tornado, trees bending, branches breaking and falling all around us, no place for shelter.

The horse and I wanted to bolt for home, away from the wind and lightning. And now, the rain, as the slant was forced by the wind, to peel my face and the horse's hide. We were at a slow gallop but both wanted to be at full pace. I could not let the animal be out of control or it would be danger in itself. The leather reins were wet and slippery, so my only control on a terrified horse was slipping in my grasp. A large branch just crashed behind me, another smaller in front. We jumped over it; the ground was slippery. We galloped on with the deafening, clanging noise reverberating in my head, the blinding lightning, the wind that made it hard to see, all around us and the feel of panic between my thighs. It was 10 kilometres of a life- threatening ride.

We arrived physically safe but mentally wrecked, the most terrifying ride I've had. Just as the storm suddenly started, it stopped. Just as I was unsaddling the horse, the sun broke through the shifting clouds and the birds started to sing. Snakes of water were running down the road and all was still. It was a typical summer heat storm. We survived.

It comes around every three years: voting. What a pain. You pretty well know it's all decided by the powers that be, preferential voting, a gerrymander somewhere, a forgotten voting box. I'm of course, wrong, it's all fair and straight forward. At Boatman station, there was a polling both with the next booth 100 or more kilometres away. Now then, most people on the land used to vote for the Country Party and the workers and union people always voted Labor, simple. But at this particular voting booth, a grazier was the returning officer and he informed everyone, "This is a Country Party booth and if you want to vote Labor, you will have to travel to Charleville or Bollen."

Well, the Labor voters thought, *I'm not travelling 100 km to vote. I might as well vote Country Party and save myself a trip.* And they did. Oh, that's not right, is it?

We were in a drought, so how come the Nebine creek

was running? As an example, we had the manager of Dingwell Station ring up and said, "We have had three inches of rain."

"What?" said the boss. "We haven't had a drop here."

We both hopped into the reliable Land Rover, to see where the rain had fallen. Would you believe that the rain actually stopped at our boundary fence, leaving bits of water running into our place. No, the rain did not stop at our boundary fence but turned around and dropped another two inches of rain on Dingwell. The manager thereon skited how good a manager he was. Argh!

It can rain further up the catchment area, that will run the creek further down. This worried the boss as the house was near the creek and his mischievous boys, who were very young, sometimes ventured down to the water. Dangerous. What did we do? We rigged up a low two wire 12-volt electric fence. After repeating that they must not go down to the creek or punishment would ensue, do you think they took notice? No, hence the electric fence.

Now, by this time, the eldest was six, the twins nearing five and little Susie, three. First, they used their little sister as a tester to see if the electric fence worked. Then they worked out that when the fence didn't click, they could get through safely. Often, the twins were causing trouble like washing the car with diesel from the overhead tank or putting sand in the oil funnel in the car and jacking one wheel up on the defender, so we got a shock driving off, not noticing the front wheel was off the ground.

We had a large storeroom for food, usually three months of groceries. The twins somehow got into the storeroom and excitedly ripped open all the cereal boxes to get the promotional toys that were hidden in them. The floor was inches deep in Wheaties, Cornflakes and Weetbix. How many boxes they opened, one could only guess. Probably dozens. It was my job to clean up the mess. We had, for months, bits of fluff and little foreign objects in our breakfast cereal.

After six months, I managed to get nine days off to go to Sydney. I had very special meetings down there. I decided to drive in one day, something like 1,150km. I stopped at Penrith, talked my way into a hotel to let me have a shower and freshen up before my important meeting. It was dusk, as I just turned into her street in Newtown. My car was forced to stop by about a half dozen thugs.

"Watya think you are doing, turning into our street? We own this street."

One of them was lounging near my bonnet, two at my driver's side window, another couple, the other side of the car. I was surrounded. I was tired after my long drive and was in no mood for an argument. In my tired, calm voice, I said, "Fair go fellas, I'm just on my way to visit my girlfriend."

"What's your supposed girlfriend's address and name?"

I was reluctant to do this but I could see no way out of it, so I told them. I was told to slowly drive up the street to the address. They followed. I got out of the car and knocked on the nurse's front door. Helen was expecting me. She threw opened the door, threw open her arms, hugged me to death and kissed me with all the excitement and love that was within her. I heard behind my back as the six hoods walked away,

"'Struth he was telling the truth."

After the joyous meeting of seeing each other again, I asked, "You are hobnobbing with hoods?" Helen laughed.

"They are our protectors. You see, they get into fights and arguments. When we hear a noise, we always rush to the windows to see the fight. Then they come to us nurses to patch them up, instead of going to the hospital. They're not bad blokes, we feel safer when they are around than when we get off night duty and catch a taxi. After some of the girls' experiences with taxi drivers, we are much safer walking home after night duty with our protectors.

Helen had some time off; we had arranged for her to accompany me on the drive back to Cunnamulla, and then for her to fly back to Sydney.

It was rodeo time that weekend and the town was throbbing. I had entered into the saddle bronc. I did put up a good ride, stayed on the wild brumby, but missed out on a place. I introduced Helen to the other rodeo riders at the back of the shutes. They just had to have a go at me.

"That's your girl Jack, from Charleville?" another rider said, "No, she's from Augathella," and another, said, "Fellas, you got it all wrong, she is from Dirranbandi." I was in a panic.

"No, no, she's my girl from Sydney. C'mon fellas, stop giving me hell."

They all laughed, enjoying my embarrassment. Sometime later, a Slim Dusty record came out with a song about the Cunnamulla Feller. And some think the lyrics could have come from the time the boys embarrassed me.

After a fantastic weekend, Helen flew back to Sydney and the letter writing began again. Communication was not the best in the bush. Sometimes we talked to each other on the telephone party line, which meant everyone on that line, probably 15 stations or more, could listen to any conversation by just picking up the receiver handle. So, the community on that line were rather knowledgeable of the romance between the nurse from Sydney and the local station overseer.

Sometimes the station I was on had a bad line. If Helen rang up, I would have to go next door, about 10km, to use their phone. When that happened, the local exchange lady would give Helen a running commentary and to all that was listening in.

"He's just getting into the car now, love. Now it's the first gate to open and shut; now he is driving through some thick scrub. Oh, he has come to the second gate," and so on, till I picked up the receiver, knowing everyone was listening to our conversation.

Back on the job, the boss and I had a bit of a contest and bet. It happened this way. He picked a big black mare that I didn't like the look of and I picked a very lively strawberry roan with a white blaze down his face in the shape of a stiletto knife. I called him Stiletto, which, the boss said, was trouble. Well, it turned out the boss's horse, now named Sour Puss, held up to its name, kicked, bucked, struck and bit. We tried everything with that horse, but it was just a rogue. A drover was passing and the boss lent the horses to the drover, thinking after days of steady work, the horse would settle down. We heard later that the drover shot it by the end of the week.

Now, my horse was indeed very flighty, 15 hands, short back, athletic looking and it took time for it to get used to me and the saddle. When I mounted it, it went crazy. It bucked a little but raced for the yard fence and just wanted to go. I yelled out to the boss to open the gate and let us out, which he did, and off we went. It was a completely uncontrollable gallop for 20 minutes before he started to slow down, I urged him on till he was tired, but not that tired. He still was pretty frisky. I realised he was an extremely intelligent horse that didn't like standing around.

I loved that horse. We were suited to each other and enjoyed the rush of the wind and the excitement of movement. Whatever movement he made: a trot, canter, gallop, turn, any movement at all, it was done quick and fast. He obeyed just my voice. If I said, "Left turn," that's what he did. Even at pace, a prop and a turn, you just had to be ready for it. I wanted to buy him, offered a ridiculous sum of money, but no sale. I said to the boss, "You might as well sell me the horse, because you wouldn't be able to stay on him, you would be off at the first turn."

The bet was made and he mounted Stiletto. We started to trot off together. The boss did not know the horse obeyed voice commands. I said in my normal voice, "We turn right here" and so we did. The boss didn't quite finish the turn and he was laid in the dirt,

I said, "The horse is mine, you lost your bet."

He said, "The bet is off as trickery was used."

I was sad. While I loved that horse, I had another love and I couldn't handle two loves at once. I also lost Prue, my little sheep dog. She seemed to get tired quickly and died in her kennel from a heart attack, so the vet said. I lost not one but two loves that gave me great pleasure. My girl, Helen, had a lot to live up to.

Here is a thing about horses; to save time, we used to put the horses in a big, crated trailer and towed it with the Land Rover. One day, a few years ago, out on the paddock road, the connection of the trailer to the Land Rover sheared and the trailer turned over. We got the horses out without a scratch, but for years after, the horses, whether in the truck that day or not, would shy and spook at the spot where the trailer rolled, refused to even walk on the road, preferring to take a wide circle around that spot, no matter what we did to encourage them. You wouldn't think the scent was still on the ground after a couple of years.

There was tragedy at Cunnamulla. It was a typical Saturday afternoon at the Billabong motel/hotel. Everyone was enjoying a drink in the lounge, when a chap, sitting beside his girlfriend, went to get more drinks from the bar. A man sidled up to him and said, "I'm going to shoot you."

As quick as a flash, the man jumped over the bar and disappeared. Then the man who now had a powerful rifle, walked up to the girl, who was sitting alone, and he said, "You cheating bitch," and shot her there and then. No one moved. All were stunned by what had just happened. The man ran outside and another shot was heard. It took a while for it all to sink in, then there was a rush from the tables. The first thing was to check on the girl. She was dead. The man didn't do such a good job on himself; he was writhing in pain. The ambulance was called and taken to the local hospital where he died a few hours later. The boyfriend, who jumped over the bar, was a lucky man and was never seen again. The girl who was shot was the wife of the gunman. The police said it was planned as there was only one shell left in the gun. One for the girl, one for her lover and one for himself. Such was life in Cunnamulla.

The government helped make the decision. The cost of postage went up and the lovers, both individually, thought, without saying it, *We might as well just get married*, and they did later that year.

It was wisely said by Helen, that I should come down to Melbourne and spend some more time together, than just the rushed two and half weeks we had actually seen each other in the last 18 months or so before we got married. (As you will see later that suggestion did not quite work out.) Arrangements were made, Helen finished her midwifery qualifications and I had given the boss plenty of notice, which was a waste of time, as the whole district, by listening on the phone, knew all about our arrangements.

Helen caught the train, from Sydney to Morven in Queensland, the town nearest the station that I was working on. And who was waiting for her with a huge smile? The train pulled up, passing the platform. Helen, with her suitcase, had to climb over the railway fence to get to her sweetheart. While I just stood there in awe. The hugging and kissing greetings were there for all the railway workers to see. We were too engrossed with each other to care.

An 80-kilometre drive on the dirt road to the station where I introduced Helen, to my boss and his wife, John and Jane Arnold, who made Helen feel at home. Helen and Jane shared the same interests: gardening and cooking. So, they got on very well together. Helen stayed in the homestead while I was in my quarters.

We had some rain, not completely drought breaking, but enough to stop the feeding and carting water for the sheep. I spent the rest of my time at Wongamere helping the boss finalise a few jobs, packing up and getting my station wagon ready for the big trip to Melbourne. That week gave Helen a slight, very slight, idea of outback life and she discovered that her husband-to-be, liked telling stories and sometimes exaggerated a bit, as well.

The first night of our trip together was at St George. We both discovered a few things that night in St George. The views, the river, the shops. Ahhh, we both woke up very happy, refreshed and looking forward to the long drive to Melbourne.

Melbourne was a safe, long enjoyable drive. We talked about everything and nothing. The station wagon had bench seats and Helen sat very close to me all the way down, which was comforting to me. But what was strange, after we got married, I never shifted from my driving position but her position changed more to the passenger side. It had been arranged for Helen to board next door to the Thwaites house while I was back in my sleepout. People would be shocked if an unmarried couple stayed together. What was the world coming to?

The first thing that had to be done was meet the families. All went well with my mother, who Helen had met before, and grandmother, and later I drove up to Marlo so she could meet my dad, who very much approved. He always thought the best wife was a country girl who was a nurse. I had to agree. We met Helen's sister, Wendy and her fiancé, Bob, at Bob's parents' place. Wendy gave me a big hug. She was smaller than her sister and had, I guessed, heard a fair bit about me from Helen. Bob was a very tall thin man who worked for State Rivers. We had a nice lamb roast dinner with the family and I knew I would get on well with Wendy and Bob. Next was a drive down to Inverloch to meet the Haig family.

C.7

Kew, Crooks, Marriage, Turmoil

I met Helen's brothers, Jim, a year older than me, who worked on the farm and Ian, the youngest, doing his electrical apprenticeship. They were fine but curious about this strange fella from Queensland, who dated their sister. Of course, Bob and Wendy had to come down to the farm to enjoy the fun.

Helen's mother had died a couple of years ago. Helen said she would have approved of me. Now Helen's father, Mr Lyn Haig, who was a tall, fit, good-looking man, at 55 years, was also very reserved meeting me. Poor man, he had lost his beloved wife, Wendy was getting married in seven months and here was this strange man going to take his other daughter. Every time I tried to make conversation with him, he would change the subject by saying how good the feed was this year and talked about the weather forecasts.

I was getting desperate; I tried many times to start a conversation. I had to do the right thing and ask her father if I could marry his daughter, and I wanted to do it on that weekend. And the father knew this and made it so difficult for me and now Saturday had passed.

Sunday had to be the day. I jumped out of bed early and

made a beeline for the milking shed, where I knew I would catch the old fella alone. I was very interested in the milking operation and was reading the artificial insemination chart for his cows pasted on the wall. As the father was passing, I asked him about the insemination of the herd and was given a brief explanation. I sensed this was the time and said, "Talking about insemination, can I marry Helen?"

He said, as he walked back to the milking, "Ufmmm, if you think you can get along together."

To me this was a yes and I skedaddled out of the milking shed, woke the girls up and said, "He said yes," There were hugs and kisses all around. Wendy said, "You only took a day to ask dad; Bob took months until I forced him to ask."

Now, after the excitement, I said, "I've done my bit darling. Now, it's your turn to tell him we want to get married in November," which was only a few months away.

We all sat around the table eating a very good lunch the girls had made. Everyone, except the father, knew what the next ask would be.

"Dad, we want to get married this November, if it's alright with you."

"That's too soon and I can't afford two weddings. You will have to wait till the following year."

It was rare that my love made a gaffe but she did this time by saying, "Dad, if we can't get married, we will just elope."

That statement upset her father and there was silence around the table.

"Mr Haig, Helen and I understand things have been tough for you the last few years and Helen and I have talked about this and we will be paying for the wedding ourselves. Helen will make the bridal gown and the brides-maids' dresses. All we ask is that you give us you're blessing and come and enjoy our special ceremony."

It's very rare that I am diplomatic but I was then. It was important for me to get on with my future father-in-law. He did not ask any questions. He never did. He just enjoyed his lunch saying only one word, "Whatever."

But all the awkward things were now done and the whole family relaxed the rest of the afternoon watching World Champion Wrestling on the black and white TV.

We had lots to do: find jobs, work out marriage plans. Thank God, I was not involved, except for my wallet. Decisions were made. We would marry at the Presbyterian Church in Kew. I thought this was pushing bad omens as my mum married there and her marriage lasted five years. We planned a reception at La Brochet, a little restaurant joining an eight-hole golf course, just up the road from where we lived. The women had fun working out the final details.

The first thing was to officially announce our engagement to all and sundry. Before the announcement, someone had to have something shiny on her ring finger. Wendy recommended the wholesale jeweller where she and Bob purchased their ring. Helen wanted a ring with a blue sapphire and diamonds mounted on each side. I was done in two respects: firstly, Wendy came along to support Helen and secondly, after Helen described the type of ring she wanted, the jeweller looked straight at me and said, "How much you willing to pay?"

That was unfair. If I had millions, I would have paid millions, but I only had hundreds and I knew whatever sum I said, he would pull out trays of rings starting from that figure. It was suggested I buy a wedding ring at the same time, just a plain concave white gold.

We went to have coffee while we waited for the rings to be resized. Helen was excited as the engagement ring was what she always envisaged. I tried to share her excitement but paying for three coffees and scones, plus the rings, it was very hard not to feel I'd been screwed somehow. But the girl was happy and that was the most important thing. That night, a drive around the Studley Park Boulevard, a stop, a cuddle, a kiss, a jewellery box, a ring put on a finger, smiles all around, we drove back for a late dinner and to show off the sparkling ring finger.

Later, I showed mum the wedding ring. She said, "Dear, you will have to engrave something inside of it."

I asked, "What should I engrave in it?"

She said, "What you are feeling at this moment."

I replied," One hundred and twenty-five dollars."

She answered with a frown, "I think you better think of something better than that."

I did.

We had to get work. We needed wages coming in. Helen, through a friend, managed a private nursing position. It was to look after Mrs Hamilton Sleigh, whose husband was the CEO and Chairman of Golden Fleece Petroleum. They lived in a huge mansion in Toorak. Helen's position was to look after Mrs Sleigh five days a week, from 6pm to 6am. A position that sometimes had trials, but she ended up being loved by that family.

I managed to get a job at the Dalgety's Wool Stores. My work times were from 7.30am to 4pm. Now if you work out those times, it meant that I would pick my darling up, take her home for a quick kiss and cuddle, then drive to work. When I finished work, I would pick up my girl and deliver her to the Sleigh's mansion. So much for the thought, if I came down to Melbourne, we would have more time to get to know each other. But the weekends were free. They were mainly spent down at the farm, which I didn't mind and darling Helen wanted to look after her widowed father.

First day at the wool stores, I was in this huge building full of packs of wool from all over Australia. The foreman said, "Wait here I will get you a truck and a book."

I was excited. I was going to be driving one of the forklifts that were shifting the bales on the floor. I studied the technique of working the machines and how to shift the bales correctly. After studying the operation, I felt very confident that I would make a very good forklift driver. I was crestfallen when eventually the foreman came back with a hand truck/trolly and a wool hook, not a book and gave me the job of manually shifting the 150kg packs around.

There was a problem for me at that wool store. It was run by the Storeman and Packers Union. Now the problem was, I like to physically work hard, use my body and muscles and do what is required of me. But I was not allowed to do that. I had to work very slowly because if I didn't, all the men might have to work at my pace.

"Hey mate, take your time. You don't have to do that, rest and have a few smokes, the job will always be there."

That advice was constant. Another thing, as I was working, someone would brush past me and whisper, "The bosses are getting their rooms painted; the bosses are getting luxury office equipment; the bosses are getting a new bonus; the bosses are getting restaurant meals," and so it went on, day after day. I was slowly being brain washed and really start to hate the bosses and the company.

The other problem was, I refused to join the union, as I was only going to be there for three months and the dues were three weeks wages. Sorry, I don't believe one should be forced to pay an organisation for the privilege to be able to work. I was warned. The stores went on strike and the company allowed non-union workers to work. There was a march to city hall; I didn't mind a day off.

The following day, I was warned at work again but shrugged it off. As I was knocking off and walking in the car park to my car, a miracle happened. My plastic ANA shoulder bag strap snapped and it fell on the ground. As I was picking it up, I noticed a row of shoes behind the side of a parked car and I knew there were feet in those shoes. I knew I was going to get a good beating or pressed into a wool bale and sent to China.

I picked up my bag, pretended that I had forgotten something and casually walked back to the store. When I was inside, I ran like the bejesus right to the other end of the store, shot out into the street, ran till I managed to hail a taxi, picked Helen up and took us home. At three in the morning, I asked my brother-in-law, after telling him about my experience, if he would kindly drive me to my car at the wool store. When we arrived, we were surprised it was untouched. I had expected windows to be broken, flat tyres and more. My brother-in-law, Alf, thought they didn't know if it was the car I owned. Guess what. I never went back and was again out of work.

Melbourne was not kind to us. Incidences happened. The first was my car was broken into outside my mothers' place. They pinched things out of my glove box, like my expensive pigskin roping gloves, an expensive torch and my very sharp stockman's knife in a leather pouch. But they also stole my silver fifty cent pieces that I had collected over the last 18 months for our honeymoon. About $35 worth or more. That was the first. You will read of another six very unpleasant things that happened to us as this story unfolds.

A new job was advertised. Wanted - driver. Must be familiar with all Melbourne streets. No heavy lifting, interviews at 8am, 29 Abeckett Street.

I parked the car in Franklin Street at about 7.15am. I wanted to be early, walked into Swanston Street and there was a queue of men. I wondered what there queuing for. To my surprise, the queue turned into Abeckett Street. That's where I was going and behold, the queue went up the stairs and into the building I was going to.

Passing all the men, I went into the office and a man was standing there. He said, "You here for the job?"

"Indeed, I am," I replied.

He said, "What time did you get here? I've been here since four."

A smart suited man walked in and said, "You two for the job?"

We answered in the affirmative. He handed us both a few papers each.

"Fill them out and I will collect them in 10 minutes."

We did and he came back and took the papers off us. Fifteen minutes later, he came back and said to my companion, "We have your details now; we will let you know if your successful or not."

The man shuffled the papers, waited till the other fella had gone, said to me, "When can you start?"

I replied, "First thing in the morning."

"Then, I expect to see you at nine in the morning. Now, the first part of your job is to go out and tell all the men queuing, that the job has been taken."

I walked out of the office as an employee and said, "Sorry fellas but the job has been taken."

There were mumbles and groans as they turned around and walked down the stairs. I did not know all these men had been queuing up since the early hours of the morning. There must have been 100 or more looking for a job. I did not know there was a job shortage and they did not know that I walked in at 7.45am and got the job. If they did, I would have been killed. The second time I escaped death in two weeks.

It was an excellent job; I could never had got a better one. They even gave me two weeks off for our honeymoon in November. Probably a reason I got the job.

"The chap is getting married, so he would be more of permanent employee."

That night, I had Melbourne city and suburban streets laid out on the carpet in the lounge, working out a formula to remember all the streets and roads. It took me just about all night, but I have to admit, I accomplished a near impossible task.

The job was driving a closed-in Holden panel van, carrying printing plates, some government and treasury, (more important than money) and proof copies of advertising literature to be changed or approved. I worked for Dovers Printing Co. and they were a good honest firm. I was one of six drivers working constantly. We each had a cardboard clock on our station. We moved the hands on the clock to indicate when we left on a job. There would be a card for the next job when we returned. We sped around Melbourne, our goods being delivered. There was a time limit on each job. If there was a traffic jam, crash or any sort of delay, that was not an excuse, the job had to be done on time.

Meanwhile, we two were very busy. I was cleaning up and rejuvenating a badly neglected garden of my grandmother/mother's house. My darling was busy in her time off. Remember, she worked nights, had to have some sleep during the day, but not much. There was material to buy, patterns to be sourced, frantic sewing on the machine, arranging posies and goodness knows what a woman has to do for a wedding. Oh, yes, deciding on invitations and how many people to invite.

Incident number two, not a bad one, but frightening. We were driving home from the farm, stopped at the lights on Warragul Road and a man rushed out, opened Helen's door, grabbed her arm and tried to pull her out of the car. The lights changed to green, I took off, holding Helen's right arm to pull her back in. I won, as the assaulter had let go, before my darling was torn apart. A bit dramatic, I know. It was a frightening experience for both of us and from then, whenever we drove in the city, our doors were locked.

The Sleighs told Helen not to worry about flowers for the church or reception, that they would gladly supply them. And I was given a message to pick up something the next Saturday at two. I had been gardening all morning and was pretty dirty but didn't bother to change as I only had to pick something up.

I went to the service entrance of the mansion and knocked on the delivery door. Mary the maid answered. I said I was Helen's fiancé and said I had to pick something up. A deep voice resonated.

"Is that the young fellow? Come in, young man,"

I said, "I have to take my muddy boots off."

Mary said with a smile, "You have been commanded; go straight in."

I did, dropping black soil clots on a thick, white, two-inch pile carpet.

"Sit here, boy."

He was pointing to the ornate lounge he was sitting on, indicating I was to sit beside him in my filthy clothes and my sweaty stink. He was a big man, white moustache with the air of importance and money.

"I have a wedding present for you. It's no good giving it to a woman, they don't know how to look after them."

Then he presented me with a black covered box with brass clips as openers. I opened it and there was a beautiful stag horn handle carving set, with the golden fleece rams head in silver on the top of the carving knife and fork. It was made of steel and was of the highest quality.

He said, "We both love our Helen, you look after her young man, she will make you a good wife."

He asked me about Queensland and if we were going back. There were a few more questions, then I had the feeling the audience was over and with the greatest of thanks I made my way back to the servant's entrance. They were nice people, the Hamilton Sleighs.

We won't call it an incident, but it could have been. If we were going back to Queensland, it was imperative that my future wife was a confident driver. On this hot October day, we were driving to her dad's farm along the Wonthaggi Road. Now this road had a tight S bend with quite a big dip. As well, there was a bridge above it, with a large support in the centre of the road. There was a speed sign which my darling didn't notice. I called, "Slow down, slow down," but the rate the car was going it was too late to negotiate the left lane and we shot through in the right lane. If a car had been coming in the opposite way, there would have been a serious collision.

We stopped on our side of the road, frightened. It had been a close call. Helen said, "That's it, I will never drive again."

"But you must darling, but take it steady this time."

"I'm not driving."

I got out of the car and started to walk. As each car went by, I hoped it was Helen. It was so hot; I was dry in the mouth. I kept walking, hoping I wouldn't have to walk all the way to the farm, with the consequences of leaving my beloved behind. With great relief, I saw our car coming. *Thank God, she is driving again.* The car went woooosh, passed me and kept on going. I had been walking for about another hour when I spied a service station and who did I see sitting at one of the shady picnic tables with an empty milkshake glass? Yep, the future wife.

We got back in the car to the farm. She was driving and nothing was said, the drama was forgotten. Well, not really. I wouldn't have written this if it was entirely forgotten.

We found a terrace house to rent in Darling Street, South Melbourne, fully furnished, except for a bed. It was just a short walk to the MCG. It was arranged that we moved in two weeks after our marriage. That suited us fine.

Where was the romance, you ask? Well, I can tell you that romance happened every second of every day. But not a normal romance. We went to dinners with some of Helen's just married nursing friends, showing off their new fondue set and new crockery and the fancy stuff they got for their wedding. Really, we only had 12 weeks from leaving Queensland and getting married. We were a busy, busy, couple.

Incident number three: we thought that my station wagon was getting old, so had better buy a later model, a HD Holden, not new, but something with 10,000 miles on the clock and only 12-18 months old. I found just the car at Bib Stillwell's at Kew.

"Oh Jack, you don't buy the first car you like. Shop around. You've got to shop around for the best deal."

Reluctantly I did. I found the same model car, same mileage, looking sparkling new with, "A Motors Dealer at Balwyn."

I traded my car in and bought this nearly new car and everyone admired it. I was just going to take my love for a drive in it, but my mum and grandmother insisted on coming as well.

Later that day, the salesman from Bib Stillwell's came around to the house. Remember the first car yard I was keen to buy their car, before being told to shop around? He said, "I came around as soon as I found out. You have bought a lemon from that Balwyn car yard. It belonged to a fertiliser salesman and it's completely rusted out, I'll show you."

He lifted the boot and lifted the mat. There was a bit of three-ply board. He lifted that and the car bottom was so rusted it had small cracks in it. He then proceeded to lift the driver's side mat and again, a bit of board and again, under the board was rust. I did not feel I had a sinking stomach, I felt it had truly sunk. The kind salesman said,

"Sorry Jack, I just had to let you know, but I suggest you take it straight back to 'A Motor Dealer in Balwyn'."

Nice, honest country lad, ripped off most of his hard-earned money by a slimy, used city car dealer. I didn't feel angry, I felt completely devastated. I took the car back. Slimy said, "You made the deal, live with it and you can't have your car back, because we have sold it."

I said, "This lemon you sold me is no use to me. I want my money back now or I can guarantee you trouble later on."

He just laughed at me and said a deal is a deal.

I said, "The keys are in the car." I left it there and caught the tram home, without a car and without savings and a lot of worry.

I told everyone what had happened. My darling was kind by saying, "Something good will come out of it. Don't stress yourself, everyone at some time or another has been ripped off by a used car salesman." Kind words didn't make me feel any better.

Mr Thwaites, Karla's father, a wool buyer, was a bit of a clever chap. He told me not to do anything about it, not to contact the used car yard, don't answer any calls or speak to anyone from that company. After I left talking to him, he got on the phone to the manager of 'A Motor Dealer', said he was a barrister from a fictitious law firm, had all the information, photos of the car and rust, had the details of the previous owner and the history of the car.

"We are sure of success of our large lawsuit against your company, we will forward the legal documents to you within the week."

I don't know what he really said, but it would have been a big bluff whatever it was. It was hard to do nothing. One week went by, another two slowly passed. Helly had to catch a taxi to and back from work. I caught public transport. What, when, will it happen about a car? Three weeks and nothing, anxiety was a constant companion. Helen wasn't worried, she never did, she didn't believe in worry.

"It does not help anyone," she said.

I got a phone call.

"This is the manager of 'A Motor Dealer'. We would like you

to come down and collect, at no obligation to you, a near new blue HD Holden, with 8,000 miles on the clock. You may have it checked out by the RACV or any other mechanics. We will pay for any inspections or costs."

I rang Mr Thwaites. He said, "It worked, that's good. Don't rush down, let 'em sweat for a few days."

I let them sweat one day. It was a beaut car and treated us well for as long as we had it.

It was getting close. Arrangements were all made, slight apprehension and nervousness by me. My darling was so happy. Did we really know what we were doing? But our love was strong and our bond to each other could not be stronger.

We were so different. Me from early divorced parents, who had a difficult childhood. It was frowned upon, children from separated parents. They just had to be immature, no one would associate with my sister and me. I wanted to succeed, be someone. I could never really relax. Work was my relaxation. I worried, got anxious. But I was terribly kind-hearted; I could talk and some would say, I could talk my way out of a hanging. I would do anything for anyone and had a great love for animals.

Now, my darling was the opposite. She had said often, "Thank you God for giving me my parents."

She'd had a very happy, loving childhood. She was clever with her hands, from craft work, sewing, art, cooking like a pro, liked gardening and nature. Helen never got worried or in a panic, everything was done calmly, never questioned anything and only talked when it was necessary. My darling was a beautiful whistler. She whistled while cooking, doing the dishes, making the bed or anything. Her patients at the hospital would say, "Here comes the whistling sister."

She was extremely strong; you would never take her on. She would be the dream wife and she loved and was devoted to her nursing. What did we have in common? We loved to make people happy and laugh. For instance, if we could not make a stranger or shop assistant smile or laugh, we were having a bad day. We would go to great lengths to get a smile or laugh out of each other. I loved her dearly. I not only loved her but admired her. What in the world was I worried about?

Incident number 4: A band was playing a merry tune from the balcony of the Melbourne Town Hall. I was to meet my sweetheart there, after she was having an interview at the Royal Melbourne Hospital for a position as Nursing Sister. We thought it would not be good for our marriage if Helen had to work five full nights a week at the Sleighs. There she was, as beautiful as ever, waiting at the lights at Swanston and Collins Streets to change. I was on the other side also waiting for the lights to change. We were all enjoying the bright music, except my love. Tears were cascading down her pretty face. The lights went green and I raced over to her, held her in my arms, "What's wrong darling?"

"I've smashed our brand-new, lovely car."

"Steady down my love, it can't be that bad. Are you hurt anywhere?"

"No, I'm fine."

"Are you sure?"

"Yes, but the car is a wreck."

The crowds pushed pass the loving, distressed couple. The band played on but my girl was overwrought.

"What's done is done, there is nothing we can do. Anyway, how did the interview go at the hospital?"

"I was on my way there when I had the prang, so I had to cancel and ruin my chances." A few more tears.

"Don't worry, tomorrow is a new day and I promise things will be different. Let's catch the tram to Clifton Hill, see the car and work things out from there."

I got a shock when I saw the car. I was expecting a few

dints and scratches, but not so. Helen told me she was going across a very wide road on a green light that changed to yellow when she was only halfway. A tram, waiting at the lights, spoilt the view of the driver who, thinking it would be a green light soon, kept speeding with a blocked view of oncoming traffic. It was quite clear he was not stopped at the lights because of the damage to our car. Then the car spun, hit some parked cars rear on, still on the spin then hit some more cars with the front of the vehicle. So, we had a well caved inside, back and front vehicle. I don't know how my darling was not hurt.

The man had jumped out of the car and yelled, "It's all your fault, going through a red light."

He was yelling and bluffing her. Poor girl, just suffering the smash and the fright of her life, to cop abuse as well. After the car was towed away, we caught the tram home to mum's place. As we were walking into the front yard, Helen turned to me and said, "Darling, I thought you would be very cross at me, smashing our new car and here you are being so nice and calm about it all. It would make me feel so much better if you yelled at me and carried on a bit."

So, I did a bit of a dance and did some yelling.

"You feel better now?" I asked, then we both laughed and it was good to see her happy again.

The car was at the panel beaters for three weeks. They did a great job, new panels and a complete spray paint. It was all done by insurance and we never did hear from the other driver. Helen got a second interview and was given the position of sister in charge of the renal ward. But we were both back to public transport until we collected the car. That was only three and half weeks before our big day.

Beside our jobs, there were still lots to do. One was twice a week to see Reverend Mackie, the minister. He was about forty something and was going to marry us. He was a fun Scotsman and a bit of a character.

I think the idea was, were we compatible or knew what we were getting into? We discussed where would we live.

"Probably on a station in Queensland."

"What do you think about that Helen?"

"I'll go where Jack wants to go."

"That's not a good answer."

"Well, it's the answer you're going to get."

"Who is going to look after the finances?"

"Jack will, as I'm not interested in money."

It wasn't going well. Mr. Mackie changed tack. He wanted a discussion, not statements.

"Helen, are you going to have children and how many?"

"We are going to have four."

"Have you discussed this with Jack?"

"Yes, ages ago."

"And Jack, how are you going to bring up your children?"

"Same way as I bring up me *dorgs*."

He was shocked.

"Helen, what do you think about your future husband bringing up your children like animals?"

A wise Helen who didn't have a clue said, "Ask Jack what he means."

"Well, I'm very interested in hearing this, Jack, please explain."

"It's quite simple really," I said. "I train sheep dogs and there is only one way to train them. With 50% discipline and 50% love. If you go a smidgen of a percent each way, you spoil the dog."

My love gave me a wink and a cheeky smile, as the minister digested the surprising answer. You get the idea of these meetings. It really was as if we discussed everything: children, money, insurance, how would we live and so on. We both thought it was a good idea and, sometimes as we walked away from the sessions, we did go into more detail about our future lives.

We discussed the ceremony, how many in the bridal party, a bride, groom, two bridesmaids and a best man.

"Will both parents be attending, and do they approve of the wedding?"

"Too bad if they don't," we both blurted out together.

"Yes, my father will but I lost my mother a couple of years ago," said Helen.

"Now what about hymns?" We both looked at each other clueless.

The minister reached behind his large chair and produced a guitar. He got up and started to play as he bopped and danced around, some rock and roll hymns. He was fun and great.

We knew the time was getting very close. They were selling poppies on the street, not for our wedding, but for Remembrance Day, the day we chose to 'tie the knot'. What a funny expression. My weird imagination had us being rolled together and tied in a reef knot. Sorry about that.

Incident number 5: We had a billiard room under the house, which my sister converted into her own private bedroom. To get to it, you had to walk down a narrow path. On one side was the high timber boundary fence with a high hedge covering it. The other side of the path was the house with small bushes in the garden. It was lovely to walk down the path to our front gate in the daytime, but a bit spooky at night.

For a short time before we were married and her boarding place was near the Thwaites, Helen stayed in the billiard room. One night...you tell the story my love.

"I was sound asleep when a slight noise woke me. I opened one eye and saw the leg of a man coming through my bedroom's open window. My heart was pounding, I couldn't breathe, I felt choked up. Another leg came through the window. I couldn't scream. I was terrified. I pretended to be asleep. I heard light steps and knew I was going to be raped or murdered. The door opened. I think he disappeared but I just laid there not moving. I had never been so scared and feeling so useless. It must have been an hour or so till I got the courage to run up the dark path and raced into Jacks room, 'Jack there has been a man in my room.' In a flash, Jack was out of bed full of adrenalin and fight, 'Where is the bastard?' 'It's alright darling, it was an hour ago, I am sure he has gone.' 'Did he touch you?' 'No sweetheart I'm alright, but I'm not going back down that path again.' Jack then pulled back the bed clothes and jumped in with his arms open. It was all the invitation I needed. I was there in his arms where I belonged."

They were all there in their best of best clothes, when we pulled up at the church in the hired executive taxi. That morning, I had booked myself into a barber for a bit of a trim of the hair and something I had always wanted, which was a barber to give me an old-fashioned shave with the cutthroat razor and the hot facial towels. It wasn't as I imagined and it made my face all blotchy, but it would be okay by the afternoon. I was nervous. This was the first ceremony I was involved with. As we were driving in the taxi, every time we stopped at traffic lights, my best man grabbed me by the arm.

"What are you holding on to me for, whenever the car stops?" I asked.

"Because I don't trust you, I have the feeling you're going to bolt at any time and I'm not going to cop the aftermath," he replied.

To tell you the truth, the feeling did come over me to take off, but it was very fleeting.

I walked down the aisle looking dead ahead. Occasionally, I would look to the left and right of me and gave a nod, but just ahead was the altar. It did not look like an altar; it looked like the electric chair I was walking towards. Don't get me wrong, I loved Helen with all my heart and everything else. Elopement would have been good as, to go through this ritual was not my cup of tea. I'm a bushman and a bushman I will be. But if I have to please my bride, I must continue the walk toward the electric chair.

I heard familiar music. I turned. My apprehension melted as I saw the most magnificent, loving, smiling angel, gliding towards me. My heart fluttered. Was this wonder truly happening? Her father gave me a wink as my beautiful, radiant bride stood beside me.

"I do, I do. Yes, I will take. Yes, I will love and honour. I will do or say what you want me to, 'cause I want this woman beside me forever and ever."

I lifted her veil. She was the only one there. I kissed those kissable lips and she responded with the warmth and love only she could provide. We were married; we signed the register; we held hands; we had huge grins as we walked down the aisle to the beautiful sunshine. We were then surrounded by loved ones and good wishes. What a wonderful afternoon.

Some notes: the church was beautifully decorated with hundreds of flowers and so was the reception and mum and gran's house. Thanks to the kind-hearted and very generous Sleighs. They declined our invitation we sent them. Later, we were told a Rolls Royce had pulled up at the church and a couple got out and peeped into the wedding that was taking place.

Helen was so keen to get to the church on time, she even arrived before me, so she had to go for an extra drive for half an hour. She has always claimed, it was the best day of her life. And as we drove away in our own polished, just repaired car, we had the cans and old boots tied to the back of it, making a healthy noise down Cotham Road.

C.8

A Temporary Married Life in the City

Our reception at the La Brochet was just what we wanted; a quiet affair with family, Helen's nursing friends and their partners and a few of my friends. Bob, now my brother-in-law, took over as disc jockey, playing good dance records. We all danced, talked and enjoyed the drinks and good finger food, excellent and plentiful.

Speeches. Helen said mine was excellent. I thought it was too. The best man stuffed his up. A couple more speeches, some telegrams, and that was it. It doesn't sound much as I record it here but as I said, it was the wedding reception we wanted and were pleased how it all went. To be honest, I don't remember a lot about the reception; I think my mind was somewhere else.

We stayed in the Royal Park Hotel for the first night and it was as good as it gets. We felt tired after our big day. I immediately took off my suit coat, tie and loosened my shirt. My bride made herself comfortable too. What we both needed was a nice cup of tea. As we sipped our tea, there was a knock on the door. *Oh no, they found out where we were and will give us hell,* or so we thought.

On opening the door, a hotel maid, holding a pink plastic

money box in the shape of an elephant, said with a funny smile, "Someone said this was urgent," as she handed me the money box.

It seemed ridiculous as I said thanks and closed the door.

"What was that all about?" asked my bride.

I showed her the heavy money box.

"Let's open it," and we did.

It was full of 50c pieces. My dear sister remembered the money I saved for my honeymoon which was stolen from my car and she thoughtfully replaced it.

We did very well that night and again that night and in the morning. When half-awake later that morning, I thought to myself, *What have I done?! It's happened all so quick. Single, then a few hours later, I have a wife.* Then my new wife rolled over, looked at me and said, "I can't dump you now."

Our thinking was on par with each other. I wonder if other newly married couples have these thoughts?

We had to be out by 10am. After sorting ourselves out and paying the hotel bill, we were on our way: a driving, sight-seeing honeymoon to Adelaide, Mildura and back home.

Not long after we were on our way, my bride said, "Stop near that telephone box."

I did as I was told immediately, as I was just married and did not ask why. She jumped out of the car, and said, "Don't sit there, I want to ring dad up."

I didn't ask questions; I was just married. We rang her dad and she talked for a while then handed the phone to me, "You want to talk to dad?"

I shook my head. There was nothing for me to say, but a slight frown of encouragement forced me to say to her dad, "I guess you got back safely and the milking went okay?"

He replied, "Yes," then silence.

I quickly handed the phone back to Helen. She said a few

more words and then hung up. My curiosity got the better of me, I said, "What was that all about?"

She just smiled and said, "I just wanted to reassure dad that everything was fine and we are on our way to Adelaide. It's something I felt I should do. He hesitated when he first answered the phone and said, 'Has Jack left you already?'" We both laughed as we got in the car and continued on our way.

It was so good. Here we were, two lovers having a great time, so relaxed with each other, enjoying the drive, the little towns and the everchanging scenery. One thing we discovered about each other, was that we enjoyed making anyone we met: shopkeeper, tourist information person or anyone at all, smile or laugh. We were disappointed if we didn't succeed. It was sort of a game we always enjoyed doing.

Another thing, when in Adelaide, I discovered my bride did not like cities, crowds, queuing or shopping. Our marriage was definitely made in heaven.

We left Adelaide early in the morning. After driving for some time we saw a man standing at the side of the road waving us down. We then noticed a rolled car down a steep embankment.

"Had a bit of an accident mate? Are you okay?"

"Yes, I'm not hurt, but could you give us a lift to Gawler?"

"Hop in mate," I said as I leant over and opened the back passenger side door.

Once on our way and after introducing ourselves, I asked, "What in the dickens happened? It was a straight road that you rolled your car on; did you fall asleep?"

"You won't believe me, but you know those big double decker car transporter trucks? Well, it must have had head light problems, so he turned the car lights on positioned on the front of the top deck."

"Yea, well I suppose you have to have lights on," I said.

My passenger continued on with his story.

"The trouble was, I was coming in the opposite direction and it was still quite dark and when I saw these lights on the truck coming towards me, I thought if that truck is as wide as it is high, there is no room for me on this road, so I swerved to the left as far as possible but eventually I went off the road and rolled."

"Is that really what happened or it's just a story?" I said laughing.

"I told you, you wouldn't believe me. How in the dickens am I going to explain it all to the insurance?"

"It's a wonder the truckie didn't see your car rolled."

"I don't think he even saw me with his lights up so high." He was a nice chap and we talked about the roll over and what to say to the insurance company all the way to Gawler.

Our next big stop was Mildura on the Murray River. A small town, we explored and did a day trip on the river in an old paddle steamer. As we were leaving the car park to board the paddle steamer, I couldn't find my car keys.

"Oh jeez, I have locked them in the car," I said to Helen.

She smiled and said, "Can you unlock the car and get them?"

"I'm an expert breaking into cars."

"This will be interesting," said my bride.

I had actually done it before. I must learn not to be into a rush and take my time, when leaving a car. Since the last time I locked my keys in, I swore, never again Jack. I tied a bit of tie wire around the back spring of my car. Bending down, I retrieved the wire and proceeded to push it up through the rubber at the top of the window and threaded it down. I put the small loop I had made in the wire, to pull the button up and unlock the door, then I retrieved my keys.

"Smarty pants," said my wife, but some of the other passengers going on the trip with us, saw me unlocking the car with a bit of wire and must have thought, *Are we going on this trip with a car thief?* It was a great informative trip but I had the feeling the other passengers were not too sure of me.

We had a great and loving honeymoon but we got back in the city of changing weather by the hour: Melbourne. Me back to my driving job at Dovers, Helen starting her nursing career as a fully qualified nursing sister at the Royal Melbourne Hospital. We moved into our little terrace house in Darling Street. As we only needed to buy a bed, we bought an innerspring mattress but no bed. We didn't mind; it was so easy to fall into bed, just a trip and we were there. The trouble was getting up in the morning off the floor, as well as making it. But the ease of going to bed was worth it.

Helen had the car for transport to work. I had the tram, but then I had the Dovers car for work and if I was in the vicinity of our little terrace house, I would call in and make my lunch or sometimes just drive past to check it.

One Friday after work, I asked Helen to pick me and a colleague up, who I said I would give a lift to. Was I embarrassed as we hopped into the car and drove off. The car had the most nauseating stink. Honestly, my throat was having an epileptic episode trying to stop me from vomiting. I don't know what my passenger thought but when we dropped him off, it took less than a second minute for him to vacate the car. I said, "What is that horrible smell? Can't you smell it?"

"Yes, it's awful, l have been meaning to tell you about it."

Once home, without delay, we searched the car for the horrible stink. We looked everywhere but could we find anything? No, until my new dear wife suggested, "Does the back seat come out?"

"No," I said with authority, "it would be permanent."

"Well, let's try our best and see if it really can come out."

"Okay, but it will be a waste of time."

She was right. After pulling, tugging and lifting, guess what. The back seat came out and lying underneath were four liquidised rabbits. The brothers-in-law must have put the dead rabbits there, as a practical joke, last Sunday when we had visited the farm. But with the car sitting in the hot Melbourne sun in January for five days, you can imagine how the deceased rabbits had deteriorated.

It took some time and very delicate handling to remove the stinking mess, then scrubbing the area with hot water, soap and Pine-O-Cleen. We left the back seat out for a week to air the foul spot. I was surprised with my loving wife when she said with a frighting frown, "I'll teach them."

Amazing what you find out about your beloved when you're just married. And so it was, Ian, her younger brother, had come to visit for lunch and Helen knew what he liked, so asked, "Would you like some toasted cheese sandwiches?"

"Yes please," was the reply.

My dear beloved placed between the slices of bread, not cheese but sliced velvet soap then toasted them. Of course, she toasted sandwiches for herself and me, with real cheese.

Ian, being a teenage boy, was always hungry and, without wasting time, gulped down half a sandwich before he started frothing at the mouth, but not tasting the difference, ate the other half. We looked on amused as he said, "Sis, this cheese tastes like soap."

I laughed at his expression when Helen told him it was indeed soap and that's what he gets for putting dead rabbits under the seat of our car. He was not happy and left for the long drive home with a clean, frothing mouth. Remember Jack, the consequences if you upset the wife.

Remember the five unpleasant incidents we were having in Melbourne. It is time to tell you about number "six".

Helen always got home before me. I was told at work that my wife had rung and was very upset, and to call her at home immediately.

"Hello love, what's the problem?"

A tearful voice responded, "We've been robbed, and the whole house has been cleaned out, all our wedding presents, everything."

"I will call the police and come straight home."

"No, I have already called the police, just come home as quick as you can."

My boss asked me what had happened as he was standing nearby, so I told him.

"Jack, just take the work car home and console your wife. Bring the car back tomorrow when you have sorted things out." I said my thanks as I flew out the door to be with my beloved as soon as possible.

The police were there when I got home. The place had been ransacked. All of our landlord's antique furniture was gone; her books scattered across the lounge room; all our belongings and wedding presents gone, except our new mattress. What was left, besides our mattress and the scattered books, were our underwear, a few clothes and some dirty dishes in the sink where the robbers had some lunch at our expense.

The two detectives said the thieves had jemmied open the kitchen window. I asked them as they were eating the apricots off our tree in our tiny back yard.

"Aren't you going to do some finger printing and look around for clues?"

They replied, "No, we know this sort of job. There has been a few of these robberies of similar patten around east Melbourne and we are investigating a particular group."

Then Helen, who knew the cops from seeing them in the emergency department where she worked, said, "I think Jack has done this, as he just took out a cover note for contents insurance just this week."

I looked at her in shock. "Why in hell did you say that for?"

"I was just joking."

"Well, that's a stupid joke at this time. I'm just as devastated as you are."

Then Sadie, our landlord who lived next door, just arrived home and saw the police leaving.

"What on earth has happened here?" as she walked in. "Oh, my beautiful furniture is gone. Why haven't you looked after my property, Helen?"

Why she turned on my new bride, I don't know.

Helen said, "We have been robbed. I'm so sorry about your furniture, but we have lost everything we own, except the car."

Sadie turned to me. "I will see you tomorrow," turned around and walked out without saying anything more.

The robbers had backed a furniture van up our little back lane and spent most of the day, loading it with ours and our landlords' belongings. The neighbours told us about it later, but thought we were moving, so were not concerned about the operation.

Helen was pleased she had forgotten to take her engagement ring off before going to work, as it was a 'no, no' to wear any jewellery to work, except a wedding band. She had taped over the engagement ring at work. But what broke her precious heart was her late mother's sewing machine. To Helen, it was her most treasured possession and she was distraught at losing it. Nothing else mattered.

We tried to tidy up what was left, which wasn't much. We stacked the books on the floor, washed, no boiled, the dishes the thieves had used and then decided we couldn't stay the night even if we had wanted to, as we had no bedding. Yes, they had taken our new sheets, blanket and quilt. They took everything. So, we had dinner at the pub around the corner, then went to my grandmother's place and, after regaling all about the robbery to my mum and gran, it was off to my old bedroom, where we cuddled for comfort in the single bed, eventually falling into a troubled asleep.

Helen went back to work the next day, so did I, for a while, as I had to get the company's car back and I wanted to ask, if I could have the day off so I could buy some essentials. Dovers was a very kind, understanding company. Not only did they give me a couple of weeks off for the honeymoon but gave me two days off to get some sort of order in our robbed rented house. Gosh, I had only started working for them three and a half months ago.

I caught a tram to Collins Street where the Australian and New Zealand Insurance company had their main office. I talked to a nice young man behind the counter. He told me the cover note would cover everything that had been taken, but he wanted a detailed list and the cost of everything taken, as well as the police report.

How in the dickens was I supposed to find out the cost of all our wedding presents? Ask our guests and friends how much they spent on us? I still didn't know what we had lost yet and could we remember everything we had owned? Gosh, that was a big problem to start with.

I called in to my mother's work, a boutique book shop, right up the other end of Collins Street, where all the top doctors and dentists were, as well as the very posh Melbourne club.

"Of course you can borrow sheets, blankets and quilts. As a matter of fact, Gran has already thought about it and probably has a bundle already for you to pick up. How did you get along with the insurance? I hope you were covered."

"Yes Mum, but we have to list all that was stolen and the value of everything which will be a mammoth task."

"I'm sure you and Helen will work it out. Remember dear, the saying about the silver lining in every cloud."

I caught the tram home to clean and sort everything out. What did we need? Thank goodness they left a kettle, pots and an old fry pan, but that was about all. As soon as Helen got home with the car, we would have to buy some food as well as a big esky and ice as a make-do fridge, until, we hope, the insurance came through quick. Yes and pick up some bedding from gran's and mum's place.

I sat down and tried to start two lists. One was what we needed to buy urgently, two, what was stolen and what to claim. The phone rang. It was dear gran.

"I have some bedding for you both and your Uncle John will bring it over late this evening in his trailer, as well as an old washing machine and a bar fridge he had lying about in his garage. He thinks they both work but will check them out as soon as he comes home from work."

"Oh, that's fabulous Gran. I was just wondering how we were going to manage without a fridge."

"He said he should be at your place at seven this evening. You will be home then?"

"Yes Gran. We are staying home. Helen is bringing some takeaway and we are going to work on our lists for the insurance."

Poor Sadie. She called around, saying, "I'm having trouble with insurance for my antique furniture and white goods. Could you put them on your insurance?"

I said I would if I could, but we had to prove what was stolen and the costs and I was frightened that we could jeopardise our claim if we did.

"I expected as much. Did the police say anything?" she asked.

"No not much. They said there had been similar robberies like this recently and there seems to be a patten. That's all they said."

"I will need a copy of the police report and I will have to try again with the insurance. It's something like, I didn't have tenants' insurance, but there must be away around it."

"I'm sorry, Sadie, it has been terrible for both of us, but as my mum said, there has to be a silver lining somewhere."

I felt sorry for Sadie, she had been kind to us and now as she walked away with shoulders hunched and head down, she looked as if she had aged years.

Helen was home. It was so good to see her, a hug, and a kiss (a decent one, not a peck).

"What takeaway did you get?" I asked as I hadn't eaten all day and was famished.

"Not much, darling. Sorry, just the good old standby, fish and chips, and we better have them now before they go cold."

Dinner at four! Goodness, it was going to be a long night ahead.

Uncle John came and we unloaded the washing machine with the ringer on top, a small fridge and some bedding in the back of his car. But what nearly brought a tear to my eye, was a fantastic hot casserole, that dear, dear, gran had made for us. Fish and chips at four, casserole at 7.30. That was the silver lining for my starving stomach.

As Uncle John was leaving, he said through the car window, "If you need anything, just holler," and drove off before we could thank him.

Thank goodness Helen still had her list of thankyous for the wedding presents we received. We wrote them out and not wanting the embarrassment of ringing everyone up and asking how much they spent on us, I would go to the shops and price everything tomorrow. Now the hard part. What did we own: first the clothes, second, the jewellery, third, cameras, radio, record player, sewing machine, etc, etc. Thank goodness I had all my tools, leather and horse gear, riding boots, whip and all my books stored at the garage at gran's house. But poor Helen had everything she owned stolen, except her watch, wedding and engagement rings and a couple of handbags, shoes and some of her art and craft work. I felt sick for my darling bride. It was just not fair.

I won't bore you anymore about our robbery except to say that Mr Sleigh managed to get the same carving set he gave us for the wedding. The Australian and New Zealand Insurance company, after our claim was accepted, called and asked if I could see them within the week, which I did. The chap at the counter looked very serious.

"Could you please give us a cheque for $25 for the cover note and premium," which I did.

Then he broke into a huge smile and said, "Here is our cheque for $10,000. Helen's sewing machine has not been paid. You will get a phone call regarding that machine next week. We understood it was extremely valuable to her."

Ten thousand dollars! Whoopee, we were going shopping! We replaced a few presents, like the electric kettle, frypan and toaster, a nice dinner set and cutlery, but the rest was spent on goods that were really needed.

But the coup de grace was the phone call we received, asking us to see a Mrs Royse at Burks Appliance in Elizabeth Street, which we did. Mrs Royse said to Helen, "Come with me, you lucky girl. Here is the latest Necchi sewing machine, valued at over $2,000, that I have been asked to give to you."

Helen was in raptures and was having difficulty saying anything. I said to Mrs Royse, "You and Burks have made her the happiest girl in the world, I can't thank you enough." Then Helen, being Helen, gave Mrs Royse a teary hug and said a husky "Thank you."

C.9

Time to Leave

A New Beginning

Helen loved her nursing job. That's what she was and would always be, a medical nurse. But I was getting restless, city life was mundane to me. I came home from work and in our small back yard, all I saw was a tangle of wires in the skyline: power, phone, hundreds of them. Then there was the traffic noise and sirens on Punt Road. And even then, in the mid-60s, I could smell pollution everywhere. I was yearning for my Queensland, the clean air, open spaces, the friendly people you could talk to and not worry who you were and what you said. Yes, I was homesick.

My love said, after I told her my feelings, "I knew you wanted to get back, I did not think you would last three months, let alone nearly 10 months. Yes Darling, when you're ready to go to Queensland, I will always be beside you, wherever you want to go or do. I love you so much."

Couldn't waste time. I bought a Queensland Country Life newspaper, looked in the situations columns for property manager positions and applied for two. I made a trunk call to Mrs Gillespie at Dalgety's in Goondiwindi, who had helped me with the job at Julia Creek, and asked her to keep a look out for any property managers' jobs, leaving my gran's phone number. Manager's job? Well, why not? Like anything I have done, I say, Jack, have a go, it won't kill you.

I bought a beaut, second-hand, heavy duty 4x8 trailer and made a light metal frame for it. One of Helen's nursing friends made, at a cost, a canvas covering. It would be excellent for carrying our new mattress and all our gear to Queensland. We also bought a tow bar and accessories, which bit into our savings.

I had some offers and interviews at Goondiwindi, after a few calls from prospective employers. I asked Ian, Helen's younger brother, if he would like a quick trip to Queensland and return. He jumped at the chance. I told him we would be camping so he needed a swag or sleeping bag (I somehow forgot to tell him the story about the snake in the sleeping bag, maybe later) and that we would not be sightseeing. It was a business trip only.

Ian and I left at daybreak on Sunday, from his home in Inverloch. We skirted around Melbourne to Seymour, then Albury and camped at Cootamundra for the night, well off the main road, after a good mixed grill at the local café. Next morning, it was Dubbo, Moree and Goondiwindi. We camped at the Queenslander Hotel, Tuesday night. We were both tired after the long trip and I wanted to be fresh for my interviews, two on Thursday and three on the Friday.

I called and saw Mrs Thompson at Thompson Boarding House. She was pleased to see me and we had a good ol' yarn over a pot of tea. It was good to see her again.

I noticed in a shop window, as I was showing Ian around the town, a paper sign stuck to the inside of a shop window advertising Corgi pups for sale. I made the enquiry to the lady behind the counter about the sign in the window.

"Yes, are you interested? I have two left; they are both pedigree dogs with papers and have had all their needles. One is a bitch, the other a dog. Do you want to see them?"

I said yes to her and Ian gave me a very strange look indeed. I fell in love with the cute little puppies who were about eight weeks old. I picked up the little bitch, gave it a cuddle and said, "I want to buy this one for my wife. How much are you asking?"

"One hundred and fifty dollars and I won't take any less."

"Okay, this little one is sold," I said, still holding the fluffy doll-like puppy, "but could you please hold on to her till Friday. I will pay $75 now and the rest on Friday, is that alright?"

"Yes, I can do that for you."

Handing the puppy back, I said, "I'll go to the bank and withdraw the money and pay you later this morning. Now don't you sell her while I'm at the bank."

She smiled and said, "Take the sign down in the window for me, I'm keeping the other puppy for a breeder."

As we walked out of the shop towards the bank, Ian said, "Are you crazy, buying the dog and paying nearly $200 for it? It could get sick or runover or something. You're mad or made of a lot of money."

"Look mate, I know it seems odd; I could have bought a saddle for that sort of money. The reason I bought it was to give it to your sister, as she will need a companion if we are going to live on a sheep and cattle station. It can be very lonely for a woman in the outback."

I pocketed the cash and went back to the shop to pay the woman. Ian slowly came round to why I made the expensive purchase, but repeated a few times, usually under his breath, "One hundred and fifty dollars for a dog."

On Wednesday, I had two interviews. One at Dalgety's office, where I had the pleasure of seeing Mrs Gillespie again.

She said, "Mr Janes, our manager, would be doing the interview, I will inform him you are here."

A very tall, thin man appeared, dressed in the standard agent's outfit: a checkered shirt with the two chest pockets, tan gabardine trousers and the highly polished Williams boots. Holding out his hand, which I gave a firm shake, he introduced himself, "Mr Alexander, I'm Mr Janes, the manager here."

We both walked to the indicated office. As he sat behind his large desk, he pointed to the comfortable chair opposite and asked, as I sat down, if I would like a cup of tea. I politely refused, as I always do. I just cannot hold a cup of tea and saucer in one hand and manage the biscuit in the other. Disaster always happens. I am usually so intent on the interview, that the cup goes to a slight angle and spills a few drips on my clean shirt or once, the bloody cup slid off the saucer and the biscuit or cake, always leaves crumbs on the desk or floor. Cup of tea, no thank you.

The position offered was a caretaker's job in the Northen Territory, which I said I was not interested in, as I preferred a job in Queensland and, as a manager, not a caretaker position. That interview finished quickly and I was told he would keep his eye out for a Queensland position. We shook hands and as I left, I gave Mrs Gillespie one of my best smiles.

The next interview was at two, at the Royal Hotel. What a shock! It could not be true; it had to be a mistake. There were only a couple of men in the lounge. One was Mr Griffiths, owner of Ardglen Station, where I had worked a few years before as a leading hand. This could not be. I walked up to him and said, "Mr Griffiths?"

We shook hands and he said, "Are you applying for a position as a property manager?"

I said, "My name is Jack Alexander. Yes, I am looking for a manager's position."

Mr Griffiths gave me a good look over and said, "I know you, where have we met?"

I told him how I had worked at Ardglen, did the mills, and bore drains, but his manager at the time, took a month's wages from me for damage to the shearers' quarters floor, which I had offered to fix up.

"I was told not to worry about it and then he turns around and takes a month's wages from me, so I left with the other employees."

"I know nothing about that, but I do remember you now and I was impressed by your knowledge and workmanship. Are you married now?"

"Yes, but only for nine months, so far."

"Any children?"

"Cut it out, I don't work that fast." We both laughed.

He shouted me a beer and then we had a deep conversation about the job, stock and managing the property. In the end he said, "I like you Jack, when can you start?"

I mentioned, "By the time I drive back to Melbourne, give our employers two weeks' notice, would a month from now be suitable for you?"

He agreed, we shook hands and went on our separate ways. Now I was a property manager, thank you very much.

I was delighted as I skipped out of the hotel, not only securing a job as a property manager, but it was also a property and country I knew well. I knew lots of people there and I'm sure my Helen would be happy in the Cunnamulla district, as they were a great group of friendly people. What was the chance? It must have been written as my destiny. I just had to ring my girl tonight and tell her the fabulous news.

I cancelled all the other interviews and now we could leave early Thursday morning and be home by Saturday. I went to the bank again and drew out another $75 to give to the lady, who was holding the puppy for us. Yes, it was alright to take the pup now, but a lecture was given on how to look after it, then I was handed a large sheet of instructions, a bill of sale and the pedigree certificate. I was told where I could buy a feed and water bowl, collar, leash and puppy food. Thanking the lady very much, I walked out of the shop, struggling to hold the squirming puppy and its paperwork. I just had to find Ian to tell him the good news and to help me with my new baby.

I found him in the café finishing off his lunch with a strawberry milkshake. I realised I'd had nothing to eat, so ordered a hamburger with the lot and a chocolate milkshake.

I told Ian I had secured a manager's job and we would be leaving early in the morning, if it was alright with him. He didn't give me an answer, as we were both trying to control a very excited puppy with food all around her. The sooner we get a collar and leash, the better.

I did not enjoy the hamburger, having to try and eat, while Ian was attempting to contain a very enthusiastic pup. I got beetroot juice on the grand certificate of pedigree and spilled a bit of my drink. It took the both of us all our concentration to control the puppy so it would not escape us. We got to the pet shop to purchase what was needed: a bright red collar with leash to match. At last, we could put her on the ground. She slipped out of her new collar and a chase became a fun/curse affair. Thank God, the door was shut so she could not get out into the street, where I'd lose my $150. Once we caught her, I gave Ian our purchases and the pup's paperwork, while I tried to carry the little devil.

I called in to see Mrs Thompson, on the way back to our hotel, to tell her about the job I had been successful in obtaining. She was genuinely pleased for me and, noticing the pup, mentioned corgis were cattle dogs and they had short legs, so when a beast kicked, it would miss the dog.

"I didn't know that," I said.

She continued that they were great dogs and that the Queen had a few of them as pets. I didn't know that either.

After leaving Mrs Thompson and walking back to the hotel, I smuggled the pup in. We started to get ready for our long journey back to Melbourne. A barramundi dinner at the pub for me, while Ian looked after the dog with no name, then I took over nursing duties while Ian went down and had his dinner. I had an exciting trunk telephone call to Helen, telling her the great news of the job and we should be home this Saturday with a big surprise. She pestered me about what the surprise was, but I was firm in my resolve not to tell her. Ian and I, through the night, had to talk in a yapping dialect to not alarm anyone that an illegal guest was in the hotel.

The trip home was uneventful, except for two minor occurrences. We were late leaving Goondiwindi; we had a fair bit of cleaning up to do, due to the enormous wees and poos a little puppy makes. Not to mention that a few items of clothing had to be discarded.

But it was the first night camping on the road and we were both tired and sound asleep when Ian woke me up, pinching my ear. I told him not to do that and turned around to go back to sleep, when soon after, Ian woke me up and said, "You don't have to pay me back by pinching my ear."

I said I didn't and went back to sleep. Then I got angry as Ian did it again. I said, "Do it again and look out."

Of course, he claimed he was innocent. It eventually turned out the pup with no name, had thought it fun to every now and then, have a bite of our ear lobes with her sharp needle-like teeth. We apologised to each other, putting the culprit in my empty swag cover.

The following night camping, after making the pup comfortable in my swag cover, we went to sleep. Now, I have a habit from camping that just before I close my eyes, I double check my surroundings. I knew the old gum tree was to my right, the small cluster of rocks to the right of my feet, the scrubby bush was north of my head, you get the idea. Well, this night in our bedding, I started to tell Ian ghost stories and frighting things that happened in the bush, not only scaring him but myself as well but, at last, we went to sleep.

I woke up sometime in the night, checked my surroundings and, to my surprise, I saw this large stump to my left about four metres away. I was sure, no, I was positive, that it wasn't there before. I was staring at it, wondering how I could have missed it, then my heart started thumping. Did it just move? Yes, the stump did move! Am I going mad? It was slowly coming towards me. My heart wasn't thumping, it was booming. The stump kept coming. Then by the fading moonlight, I discovered what the apparition was. It was Ian in his sleeping bag, his feet in the corners of the bottom of the bag with the hood over his head. He had undone the zip and had a pee, too lazy to get out of his sleeping bag. I never let on to him the almighty fright he gave me.

Dropping Ian back at the farm, I excitedly drove to Melbourne, making a few purchases on the way, knowing my beautiful bride would be waiting with open arms and inviting kissable lips. It was so great to have her in my arms again. After the enthusiastic greeting she asked with shiny eyes, "Where is my surprise?"

"It's me, I'm the surprise."

"Of course you are darling, but I meant my special surprise,"

I looked crestfallen and said, "Aren't I special?"

"Oh, stop teasing me."

"Just a moment." I rummaged around in the car and produced a white cardboard box with a bright red ribbon and bow and handed it to her. I said, "Be very careful, it's very precious."

She opened the box and there staring up at her was the corgi puppy with no name. She gently picked it up and held it to her warm cheek. She looked at me with the biggest of smiles and said, "Is it mine and can I call it Cammie?"

"Yes, it is yours and you can call it whatever you like."

She gave me a big hug and Cammie accidentally got one too.

"Darling, you're just the best of husbands; I love you so much."

We both gave our jobs notice that we would be leaving and, of course, told our landlord, Sadie. We had so much to do: packing, visiting friends, training one naughty puppy, visiting the farm and Lyn, her dad, who I got on very well with, was saddened at losing his daughter to Queensland. So much to do, days and weeks just flew. There was a buzz in the air. I was going back to my country; Helen was starting an exciting new life.

But wait for it, did you forget? The last incident, number seven. In our short stay in Melbourne. It happened like this.

I was tinkering in Gran's garage this night, doing finial adjustments to our trailer when I needed some vulcanised patches, in case we got a few punctures on the way. I knew there were some under the house in my late grandfather's workshop. I took my Big Jim torch to light the way. Walking down the bushy, dark side of the house, I spied a ferocious lion in my powerful torch light. It wasn't a ferocious lion, but the image was something animal-like and dangerous. I shone the torch into the face of a man who was intent on doing evil things. I said in my deepest voice, "What in the hell are you up to?"

He slowly turned around and started to run. I ran after him and grabbed him. It was the plastic raincoat that saved him. Somehow, he managed to loosen my grip and all I was left with, was a plastic raincoat, without an evil man in it. I ran into the house and rang the police, who had a station up the road from us in the park. By the time I started to tell mum and gran what happened, we could hear cars tearing around the streets. I rushed out to get a number plate, but they were police cars.

A detective knocked at the door and flashed a badge like they do in the movies. He said, "Why did you ring the police?"

I said, "In the last few months, our car was broken into and money and gear was stolen, my now wife had the fright of her life as a strange man walked into her room, no harm was done, except my wife was badly scared and frightened, refusing to sleep in that room again, our house in east Melbourne was robbed. Clothes have been found here, caught on the rose bushes as criminals seem to use this place as a throughfare, seeing we have a back and front street and we have found, in excellent condition, size 13 ripple soled desert boots. And now this evil person was creeping around the side of my gran's house."

"Put this raincoat on. It will give us an idea of how big this chap was."

I put it on and I was surprised, so was the detective, at how big it was. The hem of the raincoat was four inches flat on the floor. The policeman smiled and said, "I think you are lucky he got away from you; you tried to tackle a very big man. I'll go now and see if the boys have got him or what's happening. I will see you later this evening. By the way, I will keep the raincoat. Have you still got the boots?"

"Yes, they're in the garage; I will get them for you when you come back."

After about an hour, the detective came back, saying, "You are a very lucky man. There were two of them."

I answered, "What do you mean, 'were'? Didn't you catch them?"

"No, they got away from us. They jumped into the Yarra and swam to the other side."

"Well, you could have shot them or something, to apprehend them."

"Well, they could have been charity collectors and you just frightened them away. They had done nothing wrong that we could charge them with. Did you find the boots?"

"Yea, here they are, and you got the raincoat, I got nothing. I'm disappointed with everything that has happened to my wife and I, yet the police have done nothing."

"Thems the breaks. We try our best, but the crooks have their wins sometime. Could you write out a statement and drop it off to the station?"

"Yes, I'll do that, but I really can't see the point."

We moved into my single bed at my gran's house for the last two nights. It was alright, we were married. We had moved out of our terrace house, packed all our belongings into our covered trailer and back seat of the car. Yes, the car and trailer were locked securely in the garage. We definitely didn't want incident eight to happen before we left.

Dear gran, the night before, made my favourite dinner: a beef roast, followed by a wine trifle. We said our goodbyes as we were leaving early in the morning. Hugs and kisses all around, also a few tears. I went and checked on the car and gear, we cleaned our teeth and squeezed into our bed for a cuddle and a sleep.

It was early morning, cold and drizzling, the streetlights were on, the occasional house had a lighted window, as some early worker was having his breakfast. We drove through the silent suburban and city streets. Helen was cuddled up to me on the car's front bench seat, with Cammie, the pup, curled up asleep on her lap. We were silent, lost in our own thoughts. Mine were, *I'm glad to get out of this city, but then I'm so pleased and thankful to find my love in Melbourne.* Cammie, I guess, thought, *looks like I'm stuck with this strange family, but I love them.* And

Helen, what were her thoughts? How would I know, but I will guess. She was sad. She had left her family and her nursing job at the hospital and would be wondering what lay ahead.

It was strange that she suddenly woke up as we were passing the Royal Melbourne Hospital with most of its lights on. We waved and said a cheery goodbye to that special hospital as we drove on to our final destination, Queensland.

Yes, what did lay ahead? Life with its twists and turns, it's up and downs. We were driving towards the future, with love in our hearts, excitement in our souls and adventure in our minds.

The End

THE SUCKER

I was a ringer and proud to be a ringer too,
A North Queensland stockman, I was true blue,
But a Ringer was a lowly man, to the station uppercrust,
And never mixed socially with the owner, manager or such.

So 'twas a big surprise when the boss invited me,
To join them at a swimming do and, yes, stay for tea,
Well, the other Ringer's had a go, "Are we all a la-de-da?"
As I mixed with the uppercrust, in the boss's car.

I was thinking why they asked me, special like, didn't ring too true,
When the boss asked, "Can you swim well? I really hope you do."
Then I remembered the big rains up in the water shed,
Alick Creek was in full flood, a raging from the head.

Now, not many North Queenslanders can swim well, you see,
It dawned on me why the other ringers were laughing at me,
Cause I knew I had to swim that raging river, what a sucker,
To the boundary rider on the other side,
who was plumb out of tucker.

A rope I had to take, right across the other side,
So, they could fix a flying fox on pulleys and a slide,

I walked up the hundred yards, against the powerful flow,
And plunged into the foaming water, keen to make a show.

Trees and logs and a dead beast, I had to negotiate,
And the strongest current, I had ever known to date,
I lost the bloody rope as I was dragged down stream half a mile,
But made the other side exhausted and collapsed into a pile.

I swam that dangerous raging torrent, six times no less,
I was promised a big bonus and really tried my best,
And finally, I had done it, got the rope across,
They cheered, congratulations! And thankyou said the boss.

I didn't get my bonus and I wasn't asked for tea,
It wasn't a social do; they were just a-using me,
But I was happy, the stranded man got his precious tucker,
The Ringers laughed when I got back, Jack, you're just a sucker.

THE RINGER AND THE PUDDING

Oh, he was a clever one, a clever one at that,
He gets himself in with the cook, the cunning rat,
"And what's your favourite puddin'?" she's a purring like a cat,
He says, "chocolate blancmange with raisins,"
and gives her bum a pat.

Now a Ringer's lunch is squashed, flattened, toasted dry,
Sandwiches in saddle bags and subject to the fly,
But a Ringer he is tough, fair dinkum, dinky di,
And eats the mouldy tucker, with a true contented sigh.

We were having lunch on the open plain, quart pots are on the fire,
Seven hours of mustering stock, we'd done and well due to expire,
From heat, dust and burning sun, in the county of McKinley Shire,
When tickle me horse feathers, 'tis the truth, a bushman's not a liar.

This Ringer says, "Hey boys, I think I'll have some puddin' now."
"Where would you get puddin? You crazy, silly cow."
"Right here, mate," as he opened up the box,
complete with plastic trowel,
"He's got chocolate blancmange with raisins,"
we rant and rage and howl.

The cook got into trouble; the boss said no luxuries for the men.
So, no more lunch time puddin', it really was the end.
Now remember the good advice, I give you with this pen.
The cook is so important, always keep 'em as a friend.

THE DROUGHT SONG

I'm sick and I'm tired, and lonely and blue.
The sheep are all thirsty and hungry too.
The birds don't sing, there dry in the gob.
And the cattle are all covered in bog.
VERSE:
Oh, Lord send it down here.
Send us some rain, an inch or two,
or a whole lot more if it pleases you.
Send it in billies, buckets, and barrels,
To fill the holes, the dams, and the channels
Oh Lord, send it down here.
Where pushing the scrub with tractors and all.
Humping the chainsaws, the mulga we fall.
We are feeding scrub to all of them.
Oh Lord, send it from heaven.
VERSE:
The Missus' Garden is all dry and dead.
The boss is all worry, and grey in the head.
The fowls don't lay, and there is no milk today.
Our baths are dry and our clothes are high.
We are doomed to live or do we die.
Oh Lord, send it down here.

www.ingramcontent.com/pod-product-compliance
Lightning Source LLC
Chambersburg PA
CBHW011130070526
44583CB00023B/2977